Give Your Child Wings

The Ultimate Parenting Guide

Joyful Parenting

SWATI GUPTA

Founder, Joyful Parenting Club

Chennai • Bangalore

CLEVER FOX PUBLISHING
Chennai, India

Published by CLEVER FOX PUBLISHING 2025
Copyright © Swati Gupta 2025
Illustrations by Swati Gupta
Edited by Mohit Gupta

All Rights Reserved.
ISBN: 978-93-67073-82-7

This book has been published with all reasonable efforts taken to make the material error-free after the consent of the author. No part of this book shall be used, reproduced in any manner whatsoever without written permission from the author, except in the case of brief quotations embodied in critical articles and reviews.

The Author of this book is solely responsible and liable for its content including but not limited to the views, representations, descriptions, statements, information, opinions and references ["Content"]. The Content of this book shall not constitute or be construed or deemed to reflect the opinion or expression of the Publisher or Editor. Neither the Publisher nor Editor endorse or approve the Content of this book or guarantee the reliability, accuracy or completeness of the Content published herein and do not make any representations or warranties of any kind, express or implied, including but not limited to the implied warranties of merchantability, fitness for a particular purpose. The Publisher and Editor shall not be liable whatsoever for any errors, omissions, whether such errors or omissions result from negligence, accident, or any other cause or claims for loss or damages of any kind, including without limitation, indirect or consequential loss or damage arising out of use, inability to use, or about the reliability, accuracy or sufficiency of the information contained in this book.

FOREWORD
By Anita Malhotra,
Director Principal

*P*arenting is a paradox- a role that fills your heart with boundless love while testing every ounce of your patience. It is a symphony of sleepless nights, joyful milestones, unspoken fears, and infinite hope. It is the art of raising not just children but yourself, as you learn and unlearn, fall and rise, stumble and grow.

For all who have wandered in the lands of parenting and found themselves lost in its labyrinths, 'Give Your Child Wings' is a gentle light to guide your steps. It illuminates the path to a fulfilling journey called parenting, where connection matters more than correction and small moments hold immense power.

Swati Gupta tenderly captures what parenting truly encompasses: the grace to embrace imperfections, the courage to navigate challenges, and the wisdom to nurture little hearts while healing your own. Through her empathetic and practical approach, she offers not just answers but a renewed perspective- one that encourages you to see tantrums as opportunities for connection, screen time as a chance for dialogue, and everyday routines as rituals that strengthen the family bond.

FOREWORD

This book is more than a guide; it is an ode to parenthood- a journey of shared growth, unyielding love, and transformative joy. Swati's words, drawn from her personal and professional experiences, from being an Educationist, Parenting Coach, and founder of Joyful Parenting Club, speaks to the heart of every parent, reassuring you that you are not alone and that perfection is not the goal.

Inside these pages, you will find the tools to turn the chaos into connection, the overwhelm into opportunity, and the doubts into confidence. From the transformative 3C Formula- Connection, Care, and Celebration, to over 50 strategies like Golden Hour Parenting and the 7 Slots of 7 Minutes, every insight Swati shares is practical, relatable, and rooted in empathy.

Parenting isn't about being perfect; it's about being present. This book will inspire you to embrace the joys and messiness of the journey, to nurture emotionally secure and confident children, and to rediscover the magic in the everyday.

Step into this journey with an open heart. Let 'Give Your Child Wings' be your companion, helping you not just guide your child but also soar alongside them.

Mrs. Anita Malhotra
Director Principal
Lotus Valley International School Gurugram

FOREWORD

By Siddharth Rajsekar
Founder & Father of 3

As a father of three sons — a teenager, a middle-schooler, and a newborn — I've come to realize that parenting is an ever-evolving journey, filled with challenges that require us to adapt, grow, and connect in new ways. My wife, Vani, and I often reflect on the shared responsibility we carry, understanding that parenting is about more than just fulfilling roles — it's about building bridges of trust, love, and understanding.

When Swati shared her book with me, I expected wisdom, but what I discovered left me in awe. Her strategies are not only practical but truly transformative, blending science with heart to turn everyday parenting challenges into opportunities for deeper connection.

Some of the golden nuggets in this book offer a fresh perspective on parenting. Swati's approach to modern challenges like screen time, tantrums, and fostering independence is deeply human and refreshingly actionable. The activities after each chapter are unique and powerful, helping parents understand, connect, and grow together.

FOREWORD

Give Your Child Wings beautifully emphasizes that parenting is a partnership. Her book is a reminder that when parents work together in unity, it creates a ripple effect of harmony and security for their children. It's also a call for fathers to step fully into their roles as equal partners, building meaningful and lasting bonds.

This book is a celebration of parenting as a shared journey. Trust in her wisdom and prepare to be inspired as you navigate the incredible path of parenting with your child.

More power to you.

Siddharth Rajsekar
Proud Father of Three
Founder, Internet Lifestyle Hub

CONTENTS

The Day My Daughter Woke Me Up… xix
Why Do We Suffer As Parents in the Digital Age? xxiii
Why Reading this Book Will Give You An Edge? xxvii
How to Read This Book xxix
Your Free Parent Survival Kit With 50+ Activities xxxi

1. What is Parenting? 1
   1.1 The 4Cs of Parenting I Wish Someone Told Me 2
   1.2 The 7 Golden Nuggets Every Parent Should Know.... 5
   1.3 Why Bringing Up Children Is Not a Formula? 16
2. The First Secret: Connection 21
   2.1 The Foundation Years (1 to 5 Years) 27
   2.2 Middle Childhood Years (6 to 12 Years) 82
   2.3 The Teenage Years (13 to 18 Years) 131
3. The Second Secret : Care 192
   3.1 Why Decluttering Is Game Changer? 200
   3.2 A Blueprint for Growth and Connection 204
   3.3 The Father-Child Bond 210
   3.4 Strengthening Husband-Wife Relationship 216

CONTENTS

    4. The Third Secret : Celebrate 222
        4.1 Thriving as a Single Parent....................................... 223
        4.2 Co-Parenting After Divorce.................................... 226
        4.3 Managing Sibling Rivalry 230
        4.4 Grandparents and Joint Families 234
    5. Parent Survival Kit: 50+ Activities 242
    6. 20+ Strategies for Smart Parenting................................ 246
    7. Summary : Give Your Child Wings 253

About Joyful Parenting Club.. 265
Acknowledgments... 267
About The Author 269
Resources 272
Disclosure.. 274

2. The First Secret : Connection

2.1 The Foundation Years 1 to 5 Years		2.2 Middle Childhood Years 6 to 12 Years		2.3 The Teenage Years 13 to 18 Years	
2.1.1: Building Emotional Security	29	2.2.1: Fostering Independence	84	2.3.1: The Adolescent Brain	135
2.1.2: Raising Curious Explorers	35	2.2.2: Academic Growth	88	2.3.2: Fostering Independence	139
2.1.3: Play as a Pathway	39	2.2.3: Emotional Intelligence	92	2.3.3: Building Emotional Intelligence	144
2.1.4: Tantrums = Porcupine Quills	46	2.2.4: Social Skills and Friendships	97	2.3.4: The Parent-Teen Relationship	149
2.1.5: Feeding with Love	51	2.2.5: Managing Screen Time	101	2.3.5: Academic and Career Guidance	154
2.1.6: Sleep Challenges	57	2.2.6: Physical and Mental Health	106	2.3.6: Managing Peer Influence	160
2.1.7: Managing Screen Time	63	2.2.7: Nurturing Creativity and Hobbies	111	2.3.7: Managing Digital Influence	165
2.1.8: Navigating Milestones	68	2.2.8: Parent-Child Bonding	116	2.3.8: Physical and Mental Health	171
2.1.9: Balancing Boundaries	73	2.2.9: Financial Literacy	120	2.3.9: Relationships & Safety	176
2.1.10: Celebrating the Foundation	77	2.2.10: Prepare for Adolescence	125	2.3.10: Fostering Creativity	181
				2.3.11: Prepare for Adulthood	185

Your Parenting Journey

Section 1
What is Parenting

Section 2
The First Secret
Connection

2.1
Foundation Years
1 - 5 Years

2.2
Middle Childhood
6 - 12 Years

2.3
Teenage Years
13 - 18 Years

Section 3
The Second Secret
Care

Section 4
The Third Secret
Celebrate

Section 5
Parent Survival Kit
50+ Activities

*"The heart of parenting
isn't in teaching the child,
it's in transforming ourselves as a parent."*

– Swati Gupta

"Dear Parent, You Are Their World"

Every morning, every night,
When you hold them close or hug them tight,
Your love, like magic, fills their heart,
A forever bond that won't fall apart.

When they cry, when they shout,
When tiny feet stomp all about,
They may not say it — but they know,
It's your love that helps them grow.

Every "I'm tired," every deep sigh,
Every question of "why, why, why?"
In those moments, you may feel small,
But to your child, you are it all.

It's not the toys or fancy things,
It's bedtime stories, the songs you sing.
It's holding hands, wiping tears away,
It's being there — *every single day.*

Even when you feel you've failed,
When patience is gone, and energy's derailed,
In their eyes, you're still their light,
Their superhero, day and night.

So, when you're tired, feeling unsure,
Remember this: your love is pure.
They'll grow up, they'll spread their wings,
But *you'll always be their favorite thing.*

And when they dream, when they soar,
They'll carry your love forevermore.
Because no matter where life takes their feet,
Your heart is home — where they'll always meet.

PREFACE

When I became a parent, I realized that no amount of advice, books, or preparation could truly prepare me for the emotions and experiences that came with raising children. Each moment brought new lessons, new questions, and sometimes, new doubts. I found myself navigating uncharted waters, often learning as I went, making mistakes, and growing alongside my children.

This book was born from that journey — my personal quest to become a more intentional and informed parent. Over the years, through trial and error, professional training, and countless hours of reflection, I discovered strategies that helped me connect more deeply with my children and create a home filled with love, laughter, and resilience. I began sharing these insights with other parents through my social media channels @parenting_swati and my parenting community - Joyful Parenting Club, and what I found was extraordinary: the challenges we face as parents may be unique to our circumstances, but the core struggles — connection, communication, and compassion — are universal. Parenting is one of life's most transformative journeys. It's messy, beautiful, challenging, and deeply rewarding — all at once.

PREFACE

"Give Your Child Wings" is not a parenting manual but an activity workbook for immediate practical application. It's a heartfelt guide to help you navigate the joys and challenges of raising children in a world that's constantly evolving. It's about fostering meaningful connections, breaking generational cycles, and finding joy in everyday moments. The strategies and stories in this book come from my life as a mother, educator, and parenting coach, and they're designed to inspire, support, and empower you.

Parenting isn't about perfection — it's about presence. It's about showing up for children with love and curiosity, even on the days when it feels impossible. My hope is that this book will be a companion on your journey, offering you tools, insights, and encouragement when you need it most. Take what resonates, adapt what fits, and know that there's no one-size-fits-all answer to parenting. In this book, I have covered separate sections for 3 stages of child's life – foundational years (1-5 yrs), middle childhood (6-12 yrs) & transformation age (13-18 yrs). In this book, I have not touched upon infant stage and expecting mother's stage. I provide a guide for self-care, diverse parenting situations like single parents, joint family setup and many more.

This is my first book, and I am writing a 3-part trilogy in succession to this book. I will be covering – (1) foundational years (0-5 yrs), (2) middle childhood (6-12 yrs) & (3) transformation age (13-18 yrs) in much more detail in each of those books separately. If you are interested in becoming a part of my parenting community, I invite you to join me at www.joyfulparenting.club or follow my handles on social media @parenting_swati.

PREFACE

Above all, I hope this book reminds you of the power you hold as a parent — to shape a child's world, to create a home filled with warmth and understanding, and to give them the wings they need to soar. Everything written in this book is evergreen and you will be able to use them to foster child-bonding, self-improvement and have a joyous family life.

With love and gratitude,

Swati Gupta

THE DAY MY DAUGHTER WOKE ME UP...

*N*ovember 15, 2016

I came home from school exhausted, my body aching from the day's work. My daughter ran towards me, her face lit with excitement. "Why is the sky blue, Mama?" she asked, her curious eyes sparkling.

Instead of meeting her wonder with love, I slapped her. That moment still haunts me.

But what happened next changed everything. Instead of crying or being angry, she looked at me with gentle understanding and asked, "Did you have a bad day?"

Her words pierced my heart. My daughter, so young, wasn't upset with me — she was trying to understand me. I broke down, hugged her tightly, and whispered, "I'm so sorry. I promise I will never do this again."

That moment was my wakeup call. I realized that I was overwhelmed, unprepared, and taking my frustrations out on someone who deserved only my best. Parenting isn't just about giving birth; it's a science which need to be learnt.

Children are like sponges — they absorb not just what we say, but how we act and handle situations. The entire week I noticed she wasn't her true self; she was asking me limited questions. It made me realize that despite apologizing to her, the episode had impacted her deeply. My heart was sinking every minute thinking about what I had 'accidently' done to my child. I couldn't be an "accidental parent" anymore. I needed to become an intentional, prepared parent.

This marked the beginning of my journey into the world of learning — reading, attending workshops, and delving deeper into child psychology. With my educational background, Bachelor of Education and Montessori training, delving into this subject was my natural calling. While my education gave me a strong foundation, there was still so much to learn. Slowly, I started adapting my approach to parenting – pausing more, breathing more, being steady in every moment and responding to my daughter's questions with patience and love.

As I was advancing in my journey, I saw her confidence growing day-by-day. Her spark returned, and our bond deepened. These small shifts taught me a profound truth: when parents grow, children thrive.

After my second child was born, I decided to leave my job as an educator to focus on my family. However, my inner calling to share my experiences and learning with a larger community grew. I started my Instagram channel @parenting_swati which is dedicated to sharing parenting tips. Then came my website, www.atusy.com, focussing on helping children with their Creative Writing Skills.

Over the last 7 years, I have been working with thousands of parents who have shared their struggles. Overwhelmed by their own life situations, they are underprepared to respond to their child's emotions, and unknowingly pass down their own fears, insecurities and unresolved pain to their little ones. The desire to help parents struggling with such situations was the trigger to launching *"Joyful Parenting Club"*. Joyful Parenting Club is a community where I support parents in understanding child psychology, exploring self-care, obtaining practical strategies and tools, and developing a meaningful connection with their child. It's a safe space for parents to rediscover the joy of parenting!

Parenting isn't about perfection; it's about presence. It's about creating a home where children feel safe, valued, and loved. Whether we like it or not, we often default to the parenting style of our own parents. We often say that the context has changed, that times are different now. So why shouldn't the parenting style also adapt? Every child is different, and it is important to break patterns from previous generations that don't serve us anymore and consciously create new ones.

My journey led me to embrace "informed parenting" and the strategies I've discovered and implemented over time have brought immense results with my two wonderful children.

This book is my humble attempt to share my learnings with you to ease your parenting journey. Parenting is not hard work, if you know the right strategies. Its a journey of exploration and self-discovery — one that teaches us as much about ourselves as it does about our children. Trust me, there is nothing you will find more rewarding than being able to create deep, meaningful connections with your children and seeing them thrive every single day! If reading this book is your first step towards "informed parenting", let's together embark on this journey of learning and growing together.

WHY DO WE SUFFER AS PARENTS IN DIGITAL AGE

*P*arenting is a journey of learning, growing, and becoming. But let's face it – we are living in a digital age, with problems that our parents never encountered. In my experience, we are underprepared as parents to handle challenges of the digital world and its impact on our children.

Parenting today is not only about nurturing a child, but also about balancing the many emotional, mental, and digital complexities of life. It's about being present in a world that constantly demands our attention elsewhere. Whether it's navigating emotions of our little ones, managing screen time or tackling tough questions, every parent faces moments of doubt, overwhelm, and fatigue.

Let me ask you, what do you think about the times when you were younger? Were they not like:

- Do as your parents say
- Respect elders no matter what
- Focus solely on your education

- Eat home cooked food only (thanks to the limited choices available then!)
- Excel in one field only

At this juncture, I would like to compare traditional parenting with modern digital age parenting:

Traditional Parenting	Modern Digital-Age Parenting
1. "Do as I say": Children were expected to follow their parents' instructions without questioning.	"Let me explain": Parents explain their reasoning, allowing children to ask questions and form opinions
2. Respect is one-way: Children must respect elders, no questions asked.	Respect is mutual: Parents and children respect each other equally, fostering a two-way dialogue.
3. Education-focus: Studying was the primary goal, with extracurriculars seen as leisure.	Holistic development: Parents prioritize schools with balanced scholastic and co-scholastic activities.
4. Fitness = healthy food: Emphasis was on healthy eating as a part of staying fit.	Well-being focus: Physical, mental, emotional fitness, and social engagement are key priorities of child's growth.
5. Specialization: Children were encouraged to excel in one area or skill.	All-round development: Children are exposed to diverse activities to become versatile and well-rounded.

When you read the right-hand side, everything seems just about right, isn't it? A child should always have a mind of his/her own, an all-round development is a must. It is true, parenting has evolved for good over time. Yet, modern parenting has its own unique challenges. From managing screen time battles to fostering real-world connections in a digital-first environment, it feels like we are all navigating a maze with shifting walls. Parenting in the digital age is about balancing paradoxes — on one hand, there is access to endless resources, yet we have to be careful of how much is the right exposure.

In my conversations with parents, these are common problems that each one of us face, and I can bet none of these are news to you:

- Children are glued to mobile phones and laptops
    - *Getting them off the screen is a daily struggle. Whether it's a toddler watching cartoons for hours or a teenager consumed by social media or PS5, it's a constant battle. How do you set boundaries without alienating them?*
- WhatsApp is the only means of communication
    - *Connection is limited to texts or fleeting moments. As children grow, it's natural for them to seek independence & privacy. But because of the tools, physical moments together are becoming lesser and lesser, how do you maintain a bond and emotional connection that truly matters?*
- We all feel we are not good enough as parents
    - *Every parent wrestles with self-doubt. Are you pushing too hard or not enough? Are you equipping children with the skills they need, or unintentionally holding them back? On top of this, it's easier than ever to check on social media, how*

your other parent friends are doing. These thoughts can be so daunting that they can steal the joy of parenting itself.

We are working more than ever.

Between work, chores, and the endless to-do lists, quality time with kids has taken a backseat. Rushed meals and touch-and-go conversations have become a norm.

No wonder, as parents, we are stressed, anxious and losing hope more often than not!

WHY READING THIS BOOK WILL GIVE YOU AN EDGE?

$\mathcal{P}$arenting is a dynamic journey where every reaction, every emotion requires us to go deeper to understand underlying causes.

Understanding children's patterns of behaviours, reactions and your own inner instincts helps you respond (and not 'react') to children better, helping create a deeper bond between you. Unfortunately, most parents do not realize this and don't take a step forward to understand.

The very fact that you are here, reading this book, it is going to give you a head start in your parenting journey. After reading this book, you will know exactly:

- 'why' children behave the way they do,
- how 'your' reactions affect them
- 'what' you need to do in those situations,
- 'how' you will do it

Parenting doesn't come with a manual, but even if it did, you'd still wonder: *"Am I doing this right?"* One moment, your child's laughter brightens the room, and the next, you're overwhelmed by work, emotions, discipline, and the pervasive influence of technology.

WHY READING THIS BOOK WILL GIVE YOU AN EDGE?

It's a lot — quick, unpredictable, and unique — yet breathtakingly beautiful. Just as no two children are alike, no single formula works for everyone. Even twins, born together, embark on different journeys.

But here's the truth: being a parent is a privilege and a blessing. Take a moment, pause, kiss your children, and tell yourself, *"I am the luckiest person on this planet."*

This book is your companion, a guide that gives you a practical toolkit to navigate through some of the most complex goals of parenting such as:

- How to build strong, meaningful emotional connections with children at every stage?
- How to balance modern parenting challenges especially with mobiles, laptops, WhatsApp, etc.?
- How to get rid of self-guilt and self-doubt and not succumb to peer pressure?
- How to embrace progress to truly find joy in the parenting journey without being overwhelmed?

To make it easier and more fun, I have laid out multiple activities that you can choose from based on what works best for you and your children. I want you to know that you're not alone and that we are in this together.

HOW TO READ THIS BOOK

This book is designed as a handbook, for a parent with practical tips and exercises to implement in your daily life. I don't expect you to go through all of them, but I do hope that you'll be able to choose some that make sense for you and start implementing them as you go along.

Here's how you can make the most out of this book:

1. Start Where You Are
   I encourage you to read this book all the way through at least once, but you can choose to begin with the subject that resonates most with your current challenges or interests. Each chapter is dedicated to an exclusive subject, so it is okay for you to hop around and come back to other topics later.
2. Go deep
   I want you to develop a deep understanding of the problems and their solutions. The best way to approach this is to imagine an 8-year-old child struggling with screen time. Start by exploring the chapter on screen time during the foundational years, then proceed to the chapter on the middle years, and finally, review the chapter on the teen years. This step-by-step

HOW TO READ THIS BOOK

approach will ensure you gain a comprehensive and in-depth understanding of the issue.

3. Read with an Open Mind
   Every parent's journey is unique, so not every suggestion will fit perfectly into your life — and that's okay. Take what works for you and adapt it to your situation and context.
4. Take Your Time
   Parenting is already overwhelming, so don't rush through the book. Read a little at a time, and let the ideas sink in. Small changes can lead to big results. I recommend reading one chapter a day.
5. Pause to Reflect
   After reading a chapter, take a moment to think about how the concepts apply in your current situation. What stood out for you? How can you use these ideas in your day-to-day life?
6. Try the Exercises
   The practical exercises and tools included at the end of the chapters help you put ideas into action. Don't skip them! They're designed to make the concepts easier to apply and more impactful.
7. Keep Coming Back
   As children grow and new challenges arise, this book will still be relevant for you. Revisit sections whenever you need a fresh perspective or a reminder of helpful strategies.
8. Enjoy the Journey
   Parenting is full of beautiful, chaotic, and unforgettable moments. This book is here to support you through all of it, so enjoy the ride. You don't need to rush through the pages. Keep it by your bedside and whenever life feels overwhelming allow its gentle wisdom to lift your spirit.

YOUR FREE PARENT SURVIVAL KIT WITH 50+ ACTIVITIES & 20+ STRATEGIES FOR SMART PARENTING

*T*o help you in your parenting journey, I have created a Parent Survival Kit as a summary workbook along with this book. I have covered these throughout the book along with many smart parenting strategies.

Download your FREE Parent Survival Kit from the following URL:

www.giveyourchildwings.com

Scan the QR code below to claim your kit now:

Alternatively, you can use these as available at the end of the book.

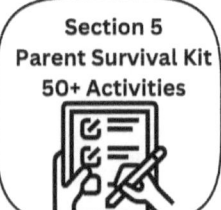

Your Parenting Journey

SECTION 1

WHAT IS PARENTING?

𝒫arenting is a journey of raising children – a path filled with love, challenges, and immense growth, not just for your children, but for you as well. While the path evolves as your children grow, some principles stay timeless. There are four styles of parenting, and to make them easier to understand, think of them as superheroes from the movies, each with their unique traits and powers.

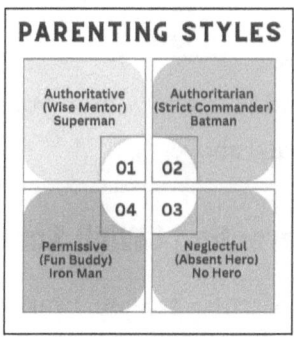

Figure 1

As you read about these four parenting styles, take a moment to reflect on your own approach. You may even find that your parenting style is a blend of two.

WHAT IS PARENTING?

I. Authoritative Parenting: Like Superman, these parents are strong but kind, guiding their children with clear rules and helping them make good choices. They always listen to their young ones and make them feel safe to talk about anything. They are what we modern parents usually want to be like.

II. Authoritarian Parenting: Like Batman, these parents take following rules very seriously and expect their children to do the same without questioning. They want their children to do the right thing but may forget to explain why. It's like, "I have told it, just do it at once. No ifs, no buts."

III. Permissive Parenting: Like Iron Man, these parents want to be friends with their kids and let them have fun, without setting any clear rules. They care a lot about their children but may struggle to say no to them when it's important.

IV. Neglectful Parenting: Like a hero who's missing in action, these parents aren't around much to guide or care for their children. They might not realize how much their children need their support and love.

What is your parenting style? Color your parenting style in "GREEN" in the image above.

1.1 The 4Cs of Parenting I Wish Someone Told Me

When we become parents, we are immediately promoted to parenting without really knowing a word about it. How much time did we spend to prepare ourselves for this new role? Possibly very little to none. Our journey starts with this new life and so does our learning!

1.1 THE 4CS OF PARENTING I WISH SOMEONE TOLD ME

These 4 Cs of Parenting were also a discovery for me, and I wished that I had discovered it sooner. Let me unlock "4Cs of Parenting" for you as I am confident that your perspective towards parenting will immediately change after reading it.

The 4Cs of Parenting are -

- Connection
- Consistency
- Compassion
- Communication

These are your anchors in the ever-changing path of parenting.

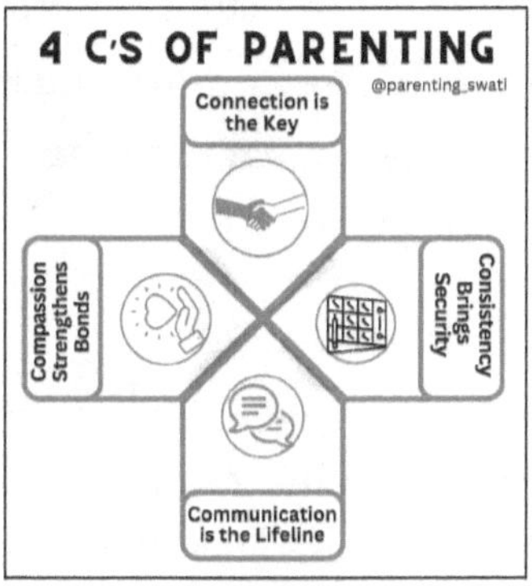

4 C'S OF PARENTING
@parenting_swati

- Connection is the Key
- Compassion Strengthens Bonds
- Consistency Brings Security
- Communication is the Lifeline

Figure 2

Connection: Connection is the key to prioritize meaningful moments daily, even if they are short and sweet. A connected child feels safe, valued, and loved, which lays the foundation for trust and resilience. A hug, a shared laugh, or simply listening without judgment can create powerful moments of connection.

Consistency: Consistency means establishing routines that create a sense of safety. This enables them to explore and grow with confidence. Consistent routines are like magic wands in parenting and deserve more recognition.

For example, in our house, screen time is strictly for Fridays and Saturdays. One Tuesday evening, when we were casually watching TV, my son stopped us and said, "No TV today, Today is TUESDAY." My husband was shocked, but I was thrilled and proud that the routines were working. Routines teach us discipline, and trust and help create more joyful moments.

Compassion: Compassion strengthens our bonds with our children. When we empathize with children, they feel emotionally understood. This can help teach them emotional resilience, which is the ability to bounce back after a tough situation.

So, when my child is upset, instead of dismissing their feelings, I say, "I can see you're angry. Let's work through this together." I try to give a name to their feelings so that they understand their emotions too.

Communication: This is possibly the most talked about but the least understood concept. When we listen to our children to understand rather than respond, we are able to process their emotions and help them better. A well thought-through response from a parent not only puts the child at ease but also makes them feel understood and emotionally closer to their parents. The way we listen and express ourselves may evolve as our child grows, but its importance will never fade.

With my six-year-old, I focus on simple, clear guidance, saying things like, "We don't hit because it hurts." For my teenager, I take a different approach by asking open-ended questions to encourage reflection and dialogue. For example, I might say, "What's been on your mind lately? Why did you feel the need to react that way? Is something bothering you?"

Now, take a pause to think and rate yourself out of 10 on each of the 4Cs. Which is your strongest "C", and which one is your weakest "C"?

> *Once I discovered the importance of the 4Cs, it completely transformed my perspective on parenting. I realized that **Connection always comes before Correction!** Inspired by this insight, I took it a step further and created the 7 Golden Nuggets Every Parent Should Know. These nuggets are designed for parents of children across all age groups. See you there! Connection is always above Correction!*

1.2 The 7 Golden Nuggets Every Parent Should Know

The 7 Golden Nuggets Every Parent Should Know is a treasure chest of insights, practices, and reflections designed to nurture your bond with children, build their confidence, and empower you as a parent. These nuggets aren't just tips; they are heartfelt, actionable strategies rooted in research, experience, and cultural wisdom.

From creating intentional moments during the "Golden Hour" to teaching the power of affirmations through simple, everyday interactions, these nuggets are meant to help you connect deeply with children while fostering their emotional, intellectual, and social growth. Whether you're navigating screen-time challenges or guiding them through personal setbacks, each nugget offers practical tools and a fresh perspective to enrich your parenting experience.

This section is your guide to:

- Building a positive and nurturing environment.
- Fostering communication, resilience, and independence.

WHAT IS PARENTING?

- Strengthening the lifelong parent-child connection through love and intentionality.

Let's dive into these golden nuggets together and discover the simple yet transformative practices that can make a lasting difference in your parenting journey. ✨

Golden Nugget 1

<u>The Golden Hour</u>

This is the precious hour before a child falls asleep — a time when their brain transitions into theta mode, becoming highly receptive. During this phase, their "YES brain" is activated, making it the perfect opportunity for meaningful and nurturing activities.

Figure 3

At home, I divide this hour into five parts:

- The first 7 minutes are dedicated to book reading and discussing life skills, focusing on valuable lessons from the story.

1.2 THE 7 GOLDEN NUGGETS EVERY PARENT SHOULD KNOW

- The next 7 minutes are for active listening, where I introduce an open-ended topic like "What do you want to become when you grow up?" or "What's your favorite thing to do on vacation?" to spark their imagination and confidence.
- Following that, I spend 7 minutes sharing important values and teachings I want my child to carry through life.
- The next segment is for affirmations and gratitude, where we recite positive affirmations like "I am loved" or "I am capable" and end with a gratitude prayer to appreciate the day's blessings.
- Finally, we share some light pillow talk, creating a calm, secure atmosphere before they drift off to sleep. This routine helps ensure each day ends on a positive, nurturing note.

To know what kind of stories to narrate, scan the QR code.

Try this with your kid tonight. Do it daily.

Researchers note that in Japan, parents have embraced the concept of the **'Golden Hour'** by incorporating calming rituals like tea ceremonies and quiet storytelling before bedtime. In India, families have adapted this idea through the use of a **'Connection Jar'** where they share expressions of gratitude during traditional evening prayer times.

Fact: It takes 21 days to build a habit, so try this for 21 days without a miss, and you'll start seeing a different connection with children. **21/90 Rule** says that it will become habitual if we stick with something for 21 days. By devoting 90 days to it, we can achieve meaningful, lasting change in our lives. This practice has been around for centuries but was famously outlined in the book Psycho-Cybernetics by Maxwell Malt.

Golden Nugget 2

DEAR (Drop Everything and Read) Time

It is a simple yet powerful habit that encourages both kids and adults to read more. Set an alarm for DEAR time every night, and when the alarm rings, the whole house should pause all activities and dedicate uninterrupted time to reading. This practice helps build a lifelong love for books while improving vocabulary, comprehension, and focus. When parents read alongside their children, it reinforces the importance of reading as a shared, enriching experience.

If the child is below reading age, give them picture books instead. Picture books can help kids grow their imagination and improve their interpretation skills.

For Age-wise Book Recommendations, scan the QR Code!

Golden Nugget 3
The Hidden Message of Water in our Body

Did you know that water holds hidden messages? Water crystals respond to emotions, words, and intentions, and even have memory. Positive stimuli, such as kind words or prayers, create stunning, harmonious crystals, while negative words or harsh tones result in chaotic, distorted ones.

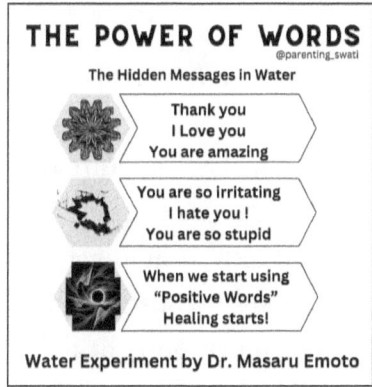

Figure 4

Now consider this: the human body is made up of 75% water, and the brain relies heavily on it. This means our words and emotions can impact us at a molecular level. It also underscores the power of affirmations, especially when speaking to children. Casual remarks like "stupid" or "silly" might seem harmless to us, but they can leave lasting imprints on a child's self-esteem and mental well-being.

Children absorb everything. Positive affirmations — expressing love, encouragement, and belief in their abilities — help foster confidence, resilience, and healthy emotional development.

Dr. Masaru Emoto's research serves as a powerful reminder that our words not only influence water crystals but also shape the emotional and psychological landscapes of those around us, particularly children. Choose your words wisely — they hold the power to transform.

WHAT IS PARENTING?

Get a list of Age-Wise Affirmations by scanning the QR code.

Golden Nugget 4
Stop Labeling Children in Public

Recently, I attended a birthday party with my son. Since he didn't know most of the people there, he chose to sit beside me. A few mothers at another table commented, "Oh, he's shy, isn't he?" I immediately corrected them and said, "No, not at all. He's observant. He takes his time to understand his surroundings, but once he's comfortable, he confidently makes friends." His face lit up listening to this, and to all our pleasant surprise, he began playing with everyone comfortably.

What we say becomes their inner voice! So, when you label children as "shy," "naughty," "lazy," "thin," "fat," or "dark," their subconscious mind is listening — and believing it. The subconscious brain shapes their identity, and over time, they start thinking, *"This is who I am, and I can't change." So, try saying this instead...*

Naughty = Curious
Quiet = Calm
Hyperactive = Energetic
Messy = Creative
Bossy = Confident
Dramatic = Expressive

1.2 THE 7 GOLDEN NUGGETS EVERY PARENT SHOULD KNOW

Difficult = Independent
Messy = Creative
Impulsive = Spontaneous
Quiet = Thoughtful
Clingy = Loving
Sensitive = Empathetic

These labels limit their growth, making them feel stuck in a fixed mindset. So, as parents we should focus on positive reinforcement and encourage growth. Let your words shape their potential, not limit it.

Golden Nugget 5

Screen Time and Popcorn Brain in Kids

Research shows that children under 7 spend over 4 hours/day on screens, while kids 7–14 years of age average 7.7 hours of screen time per day, often watching reels and high-stimulus videos. This overstimulation, called "Popcorn Brain," overwhelms their underdeveloped nervous system, leading to tantrums, speech delays, aggression, difficulty focusing and low creativity.

As parents, we should prioritize low-stimulation content such as educational videos, pretend play guidance, and vocabulary-building resources. In my household, podcasts like *Baalgatha* and *The Kahani Project* have been particularly effective. They not only spark my child's imagination but also enhance focus by encouraging the creation of mental imagery. Additionally, little ones enjoys interactive activities like quizzes and math-based questions through "ALEXA," making learning both fun and engaging.

WHAT IS PARENTING?

Golden Nugget 6

<u>The 7 Slots of 7 Minutes</u>

This is a concept I created after observing and analyzing the ideal times to spend with the kids. Whether you are a working parent or stay-at-home parent we all struggle with time. The good news is, building a strong connection doesn't take hours. Just 7 slots of 7 minutes each day can work wonders.

7 SLOTS OF 7 MINUTES
@parenting_swati
- ◯ Morning Hugs and Affirmation
- ◯ Breakfast and Story Telling
- ◯ After School Connection
- ◯ FREE Outdoor Play + Classes
- ◯ Dinner Bonding Time
- ◯ Emotional Coaching at Night
- ◯ Gratitude Prayer + Affirmations

Figure 5

Let me break it for you on how I do it in my house

1. Morning Moment: We start the day with a smile, a hug, an affirmation song, which charges our day.
2. Drop-Off Connection: We share a quick affirmation and go over the classes for the day so that our expectations are matched.
3. Post-School Check-In: Listen to their highs and lows with your full attention and enjoy their conversation.

4. Dinner Table Delight: We chat about the day or play a simple conversation game with loads of laughter.
5. Bedtime Bonding: We end the day with cuddles, an affirmation, a story and some pillow talk.
6. The Bonus Slot: I combine 2 slots together for my Golden Hour conversation.
7. Spontaneous Moments: A high-five, a shared laugh, or exchanging a simple "I love you" during the day.

These 49 minutes of focused moments daily add up to big, lasting bonds. You don't need to do it perfectly — just consistently. But remember to keep the moments devoid of any gadgets.

Golden Nugget 7

The Power of Sharing Personal Challenges with Children

When I was preparing for my Josh Talk, I was incredibly nervous. I confided in my daughter about my feelings, and together, we practiced a calming technique. She hugged me, offering her support, and that simple moment gave me the strength I needed.

Sharing such vulnerable moments with your children teaches them that it's okay to feel scared, nervous, or uncertain — it's part of being human. By opening up about your own challenges, you show them that vulnerability is not a weakness but a stepping stone to growth.

We demonstrate resilience by bouncing back, taking charge, and overcoming obstacles. These shared experiences convey that tough times are temporary and can lead to strength and confidence. When children see you embrace your emotions, they internalize the lesson that they too can face their challenges with a "bounce-back" mindset, emerging stronger every time.

Parenting is deeply influenced by culture, traditions, and societal expectations. These strategies are meant to compliment your values and beliefs, not replace them.

PRO TIP: Parenting is not about having all the answers. Seeking guidance — whether from books, professionals, or a supportive community — is a strength, not a weakness. You can check out my website www.joyfulparenting.club for information about 1:2:1 consultation, Parenting Masterclass and much more.

The Role of Boundaries: Freedom Within Limits

By now you would have understood that I like boundaries in my house. Boundaries are not barriers, they're guideposts that provide children safety, structure, and a foundation for healthy exploration. Imagine pouring water into an open space — it spreads out aimlessly and becomes unmanageable. But pour the same water into a large bowl, and it becomes contained, visible, and purposeful.

Boundaries work the same way: they channel a child's energy in a direction that fosters security, discipline, and independence, while still giving them the freedom to discover who they are within safe limits. They empower children to thrive, not restrict them.

Guided Reflection for Parents

Take a moment to reflect on your journey:
- What's one parenting moment that made you proud this week?
- How have you grown as a parent since your child was born?

- What's one small change you can make to strengthen your connection with children?

The Bigger Picture: Connection Over Correction

Every tantrum, every hug, every "why?" is an opportunity to connect, guide, and grow.

Use these MAGIC MOMENTS to Connect with Children

1. Morning: Start their day with positivity — offer a hug or kind words to set a cheerful tone.
2. After School: Show interest in their day — ask open-ended questions and listen attentively.
3. Before Bed: End with love — share cuddles, stories, or affirmations to reassure and comfort them.

Sample Checklist

Activity	Completed?
Morning hug	Yes/No
Storytime before bed	Yes/No
Talking about feelings	Yes/No
Sharing affirmations	Yes/No
Encouraging positive behavior	Yes/No

Parenting is one of life's most beautiful adventures. Every misstep is an opportunity to learn — for both you and your child. Love, patience, and the 4C's are your most powerful tools. Together, let's embrace this journey. You've got this, and this book is here to support you every step of the way. Let's now talk about the Parenting SECRET SAUCE.

WHAT IS PARENTING?

1.3 Why Bringing Up Children Is Not a Formula?

Parenting is a wild ride! One moment you're the superhero who knows all the answers, and the next, you're Googling "how to get a toddler to eat vegetables" or "why does my teenager roll their eyes so much." It's messy, chaotic, and beautiful all at once. But what if I told you that <u>three simple secrets</u> could make it all feel just a little easier?

These three secrets aren't about perfection — they're about making the journey meaningful, joyful, and just a little less overwhelming. These 3 secrets are like the house built on the 4 pillars of parenting, so both are interlinked with each other.

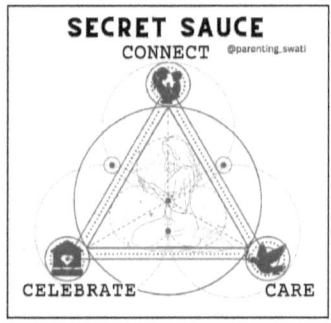

Figure 6

Secret 1: Connect

Here's the thing: every child, whether they're two or seventeen, just wants to feel loved and understood. Connection is the foundation of everything. It's the glue that keeps you and your child close, even when life gets hectic or challenging.

1.3 WHY BRINGING UP CHILDREN IS NOT A FORMULA?

Think about it — behind every tantrum, slammed door, or grumpy "I'm fine" is a little human who just wants to know, "Are you here for me?" Connection is about answering that question, again and again, with your actions, your words, and your presence.

It doesn't have to be complicated. A hug before bedtime, a laugh over a silly joke while dropping them to school, or a real "I'm listening" moment during the car ride while coming back home from school can work wonders. It's not about how much time you spend; it's about how you spend it.

Connection isn't about fixing your child's problems — it's about being there while they figure things out. And as you'll see in this book, connecting with children at every stage is the secret sauce to navigating tantrums, friendships, mood swings, and everything in between.

Secret 2: Care

Okay, parents, let's get real for a second. You've got a million things on your plate — work, house chores, school drop-offs, and let's not forget the endless snack requests. Somewhere in the chaos, you've probably forgotten one important person: YOU.

But here's the truth: a happy parent raises a happy child. When you're running on fumes, it's hard to show up as your best self. That's where Care comes in. And no, this isn't about bubble baths and spa days (though if you can squeeze those in, go for it). Self-care is about giving yourself permission to pause, breathe, and refuel.

Think of it like this: you can't pour from an empty cup. When you take care of yourself — whether it's sneaking in five minutes of quiet coffee time or going for a quick walk — you're actually taking care of your whole family. Because a rested, energized, and happy parent is the best gift you can give children.

Self-care is not selfish — it's SELF-ISHQ. It's not about indulgence — it's about survival. And most importantly, it's about modelling balance for your kids. After all, wouldn't you want them to grow up knowing how to take care of themselves, too?

Secret 3: Celebrate

Now for the fun part: Celebrate. This is where parenting becomes less about surviving and more about thriving.

Celebrate isn't just about big milestones — though those are great. It's about noticing and cherishing the small, everyday moments that make your family unique. It's the *aloo ka parantha* breakfast, the family dance parties and the hugs after a long day. These moments may seem ordinary, but they're the ones your kids will remember forever.

But it's not just about the kids. Celebrate your journey as a parent. Celebrate your family's quirks — whether you're a single parent, co-parenting, part of a joint family, or a nuclear family or figuring out your own unique dynamic. Every family looks different, and that's worth honouring. Joy is the glue that keeps families strong. And trust me, even in the hardest moments, there's always something worth celebrating.

Putting It All Together: Connect. Care. Celebrate.

These three secrets are simple, but they're powerful.

1.3 WHY BRINGING UP CHILDREN IS NOT A FORMULA?

- Connect with children deeply
- Care of yourself unapologetically, and
- Celebrate your family wholeheartedly.

Together, they form the foundation of joyful, resilient parenting.

So, let's dive in, embrace the mess, and uncover the magic of *Connect, Care, Celebrate*. First, we will dive deep into Connect. Our little ones are the most beautiful thing happen to us, so let's decode how to "Connect" with our little ones better.

Section 1
What is Parenting

YOU ARE HERE

Section 2
The First Secret
Connection

2.1
Foundation Years
1 - 5 Years

2.2
Middle Childhood
6 - 12 Years

2.3
Teenage Years
13 - 18 Years

Section 3
The Second Secret
Care

Section 4
The Third Secret
Celebrate

Section 5
Parent Survival Kit
50+ Activities

Your Parenting Journey

SECTION 2

THE FIRST SECRET: CONNECTION

Connection is above Correction!

*P*arenting is a journey like no other — messy, magical, challenging, and rewarding all at once. The key to thriving? Connection – which is the foundation of parenting.

Connection occurs during the hug that soothes a tantrum, the conversations that bridge distance with your teenager, and the small, everyday moments that say, "I see you, and I'm here." When you're connected to your children, everything else — discipline, guidance, and teaching — falls into place.

As children grow, so does your role as a parent. From their first steps to their first big milestones, you'll transition from nurturer to coach to confidant. Yet, through every stage, connection remains the constant thread that strengthens your bond and helps children flourish. You're not just raising a child — you're building a lifelong relationship.

THE FIRST SECRET: CONNECTION

In this section, we'll explore the evolving power of connection and why it's the cornerstone of everything in parenting. I have divided connection into 3 sections -

- **The Foundational Stage from 1 to 5 years**- This is the age of firsts: first steps, first words, first everything. You're their whole world, their safe place. Connection here means giving them a strong sense of security.
- **The Growth Stage from 6 to 12 years**- Middle childhood is where curiosity takes flight. They start to explore their independence, but they still need you to be their steady guide. Connection at this stage means showing up as their biggest supporter while letting them stretch their wings. This section is divided into 2 parts -Early growth years (6-8 Years) and Pre-teens (9-12 Years).
- **The Transformational Stage from 13 to 19 years**- Ah, the teenage years — a roller coaster of emotions, independence, and figuring out who they are. Connection here means being their anchor, even when they push you away. They need to know you're there, ready to listen without judgment.

Why Connection Matters

Connection is the first secret sauce to parenting. When children feel truly connected to you, they're more open to learning, growing, and cooperating. It's what builds trust, fosters resilience, and creates a home filled with love.

But let's be clear – connection isn't about grand gestures. It's not about crafting the perfect family game night or taking exotic vacations. It's about the small, everyday moments:

- A hug in the morning.
- Laughing together at a silly joke.
- Listening when they tell you about their day, even if it's just about Minecraft or math homework.

These little moments add up to something big. They say to children, "You matter to me."

The Changing Role of Connection

As children grow, your connection with them will evolve.

- The Nurturer (1–5 Years): You're their everything — their protector, comforter, and biggest cheerleader.
- The Coach (6–12 Years): You're teaching them how to navigate the world while cheering them on from the sidelines.
- The Advisor (13–19 Years): You're their trusted guide, helping them make sense of life's big questions while giving them the freedom to explore.

Your role may change, but your connection will always be the foundation. Let me elaborate on what we will cover in The First Secret – Connect.

THE FIRST SECRET: CONNECTION

2. The First Secret : Connection

2.1 The Foundation Years 1 to 5 Years		2.2 Middle Childhood Years 6 to 12 Years		2.3 The Teenage Years 13 to 18 Years	
2.1.1: Building Emotional Security	29	2.2.1: Fostering Independence	84	2.3.1: The Adolescent Brain	135
2.1.2: Raising Curious Explorers	35	2.2.2: Academic Growth	88	2.3.2: Fostering Independence	139
2.1.3: Play as a Pathway	39	2.2.3: Emotional Intelligence	92	2.3.3: Building Emotional Intelligence	144
2.1.4: Tantrums = Porcupine Quills	46	2.2.4: Social Skills and Friendships	97	2.3.4: The Parent-Teen Relationship	149
2.1.5: Feeding with Love	51	2.2.5: Managing Screen Time	101	2.3.5: Academic and Career Guidance	154
2.1.6: Sleep Challenges	57	2.2.6: Physical and Mental Health	106	2.3.6: Managing Peer Influence	160
2.1.7: Managing Screen Time	63	2.2.7: Nurturing Creativity and Hobbies	111	2.3.7: Managing Digital Influence	165
2.1.8: Navigating Milestones	68	2.2.8: Parent-Child Bonding	116	2.3.8: Physical and Mental Health	171
2.1.9: Balancing Boundaries	73	2.2.9: Financial Literacy	120	2.3.9: Relationships & Safety	176
2.1.10: Celebrating the Foundation	77	2.2.10: Prepare for Adolescence	125	2.3.10: Fostering Creativity	181
				2.3.11: Prepare for Adulthood	185

A Quick Reality Check

Not every moment will feel magical. Some days will be full of missed connections, misunderstandings, and meltdowns (theirs and yours). That's okay. Connection isn't about getting it right all the time. It's about showing up, being present, and saying, "I'm here, even when it's hard."

Remember: Less is More... Don't stop or correct your child all the time. Your kids might start selective listening and ignore the rest of what you say.

As we move forward, we'll explore how to nurture connection at every stage of children's growth. You'll learn practical ways to build trust, foster communication, and create a home filled with warmth and love.

Remember: connection is the starting point. It's the foundation of everything else in parenting — and it's where the real magic happens.

Let's take it one step, one hug, one laugh at a time. ✨

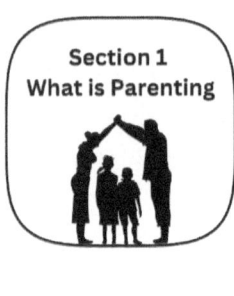

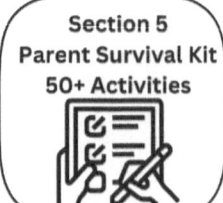

Your Parenting Journey

2.1 The Foundation Years (1 to 5 Years)

Welcome to the foundation years — a wild, wonderful ride of growth, giggles, and plenty of "why?" questions. These are the years when your little one is discovering the world (and testing every boundary in it), and you're discovering the joys and chaos of parenthood. It's messy. It's magical. And it's the foundation for everything to come.

These years shape children's emotional security, social skills, and love of learning. Your role? To guide, nurture, and occasionally just survive the day. Some days feel like you've nailed it; others are a blur of tantrums, snacks, and bedtime negotiations.

Let's dive into the joys and challenges of this phase and figure it out together.

The Real Challenges of the Foundation Years

Parenting toddlers and preschoolers is equal parts privilege and exhaustion. Here's what you're probably juggling (and yes, it's normal):

1. Exhaustion is your middle name- Feeding, chasing, soothing, repeat. You're always on the go, physically and emotionally. You're not just raising a tiny human; you're running a full-time operation.
2. Tantrum central- Their favorite cup isn't clean, or their sock feels "weird." Cue the meltdown. It's not rebellion — it's just big feelings in a tiny body. And yes, it's exhausting.
3. The comparison trap- Is your toddler behind on walking? Should they be eating kale instead of crackers? Social media and playground gossip can make you feel like you're falling

THE FIRST SECRET: CONNECTION

short. Here's the truth: every child's path is unique, and so is yours.

4. Walking the freedom-tantrum tightrope- They want independence but have zero clue about consequences. Letting them explore without letting them break the house? It's an art form.
5. No time for yourself- Remember hobbies? Sleep? Showering without interruptions? Self-care feels like a luxury, but it's actually a necessity. A happy parent raises a happy kid.
6. Food fights- One day they love broccoli; the next, it's their sworn enemy. Feeding battles can make mealtime feel like a war zone. Trust me — you're not alone.
7. Milestone mania- First steps, first words, first everything. Milestones are exciting but can also trigger anxiety. Relax. Growth isn't a race, and children are on their own timeline.
8. Screens and socializing- How much screen time is too much? Are they making enough friends? These questions loom large, but balance is more achievable than you think.
9. Managing work and kids – For working moms and dads, its tough. And finding nannies and trusting them is even tougher.

Take a breath. You're an awesome parent. Pat on your back for reading this book so that you can make a difference in yours and your child's life.

In the section ahead, we'll tackle these challenges together. You'll learn –

1. How to build emotional security?
2. How to raise curious explorers?
3. How is play a pathway to growth?

4. How to handle tantrums?
5. How to survive mealtime battles?
6. How to overcome sleep challenges?
7. How to manage screen time in digital age?
8. How to navigate milestones at every step?
9. How to balance boundaries?
10. How can we celebrate foundational years?

And together, we'll make these foundation years unforgettable — for all the right reasons. Let's get started!

2.1.1: Building Emotional Security

Hello, parents! Let's kick things off with something fundamental yet profoundly impactful: emotional security. Think of it as the cornerstone of children's lifelong growth — the firm ground that allows them to face the world with courage, resilience, and an open heart. During these formative years, your little one depends on you to help them navigate big emotions and the sometimes-overwhelming landscape of their growing world.

Here's the good news: You don't need to be perfect (Spoiler alert: Nobody is!) What truly matters is showing up consistently with love, patience, and understanding. And remember, you're not alone in this journey — I'm here with you, offering encouragement, tools, and guidance every step of the way. Together, we'll build a foundation that will shape not only children's future but also your bond with them.

The bond between you and your child creates a "secure base". This base is a safe, loving space from which children can explore the world, take risks, and come back for comfort when needed. When children know they can count on you, they feel safe enough to try new things, face challenges, and develop healthy relationships. Think of yourself as their home port in a busy harbour — they can always return to you for love and reassurance, no matter how stormy the seas of life may get.

Before kids can manage their own big feelings, they rely on you to help them process emotions. This is called <u>co-regulation</u>. For example, when your toddler has a meltdown, your calm voice, soothing touch, and reassurance help them calm down. Over time, your support teaches them how to handle emotions independently. Think of it as training wheels for emotional intelligence.

Best way to build emotional security is through **'Rituals & Routines'**. It helps the child predict what to expect and makes them feel grounded and connected:

1. Morning rituals: A cheerful "Good morning, sunshine," followed by brushing teeth, getting dressed, and a quick snuggle can set a positive tone for the day.

Pro tip: Add a playful touch, like a "special handshake" or a dance party while getting ready. We have a special affirmation song which we sing daily and dance on it with actions. It helps to release "Oxytocin", which means that their happy brain is activated.

Our Affirmation Song-
> *"I am strong, I am powerful, I am amazing inside.*
> *I am kind, I am mindful, I am Mumma's Sunshine.*
> *I am happy, I am lucky, I speak my mind.*
> *I am a happy, happy, happy child...I love my life!"*

2.1 THE FOUNDATION YEARS (1 TO 5 YEARS)

Did You Know? When you tell your children, "You are strong" or "You are loved," their 37 trillion cells respond to that affirmation. You're literally wiring their brain for security and self-worth.

2. Mealtime Routines: Create little traditions like saying what you're thankful for before dining or letting children pick one "special" food for the meal. Example: "Let's set the table together. You can be in charge of napkins!"
3. Transition Rituals: Help children adjust to changes (like leaving the park or starting daycare) with predictable cues. A goodbye song or hug-and-wave routine can make transitions smoother.

There are common parenting challenges that I notice at this age, and we need to tackle them with the emotional security of your child in mind:

1. Clinginess: It's totally normal for children to not want to let go of you when they're being dropped off. Reassure them by establishing a consistent goodbye ritual. Inform them and keep it simple, "I'll hug you, then wave from the door, and I'll see you after snack time!" Talk about it during the golden hour and tell them how much fun it is to go to school.
2. Sibling Rivalry: Your toddler snatches a toy from their older sibling, triggering World War III? Instead of refereeing, acknowledge both kids' feelings. Tell them "You both want the truck, and that's hard. Let's take turns. Who wants to go first?" I have covered the whole section on sibling rivalry in The Third Secret in Section 4.3 – don't miss it!
3. Tantrums in Public: Your child lies down in the middle of the grocery store because they want something which you told

THE FIRST SECRET: CONNECTION

them you can't give. If this happens, you need to stay calm, kneel down, and validate their feelings. Tell them "I know you're upset because we can't get cookies. It's okay to feel mad. Let's take deep breaths together." Remember the golden nugget where we covered this?

Another challenge is faced by working parents, who often struggle with stress and guilt. Being a single parent or a working parent is undoubtedly tough, and time always seems to be in short supply. However, it's important not to stress too much. Emotional security for children isn't about being present every moment; it's about making the moments you are present truly meaningful and impactful.

Here's how to maximize quality time

1. Micro-Moments of Connection: Remember the Golden Nugget - 7 Slots of 7 Minutes? That really works. Even a 7-minute cuddle or singing a silly song during the drive to daycare can make a big impact. Discuss "Let's see how many animals we can name before we get there!"
2. Lean on Rituals: Consistency is your best friend. Even if you're juggling a packed schedule, routines like Golden hour or a goodbye hug can reassure children that they're loved.

Tag Team with Your Village: Rely on supportive caregivers, family, or friends. You don't have to do it all alone. Asking for help is your power and not your weakness. Hiring a nanny is also an option worth exploring.

1. Managing nannies can be tricky and is a serious business. Choose the Right Nanny: Select someone who aligns with

your parenting values and routines. Conduct thorough reference checks and start with a trial period.
2. Set Clear Expectations: Provide detailed guidelines on routines, discipline, and communication. Regular check-ins ensure consistency and trust.
3. Collaborate and Empower: Encourage the nanny to engage in meaningful activities like storytelling or crafts while maintaining key "parent-only" moments for bonding.
4. Establish Routines: Use shared rituals like "Golden Hour" for emotional security. The nanny can assist with these routines in your absence.
5. Maximize Quality Time: Focus fully on children during micro-moments like bedtime stories or quick games. Even short, intentional interactions matter.
6. Leverage Support Networks: Coordinate with family and ensure the nanny keeps you updated on children's milestones and activities.

Remember, it's about quality over quantity. With clear communication and shared routines, you can create a nurturing environment for children.

Activity: The Connection Jar

This builds a stronger bond with your children through shared moments of love and gratitude.

THE FIRST SECRET: CONNECTION

Figure 7

How It Works

1. Grab a jar and slips of paper. Call it your Connection Jar.
2. Each day, write one moment you loved, like:
   - *"I loved our bedtime snuggle."*
   - *"You made me smile when you shared your toys!"*
3. Once a month, read the notes together and relive those special moments.

This simple ritual helps children feel loved, seen, and appreciated while deepening your bond. Do this activity whenever your children put a smile on your face.

Take a deep breath. You're doing an amazing job. Whether it's one more bedtime hug, a quick smile of encouragement, or a heartfelt "I'm proud of you," you're shaping your children's world in incredible ways.

Together, we've got this. ♡

2.1.2: Raising Curious Explorers

Now, let's dive into one of the most magical parts of early childhood: curiosity. Children are natural explorers, like scientists who are constantly testing, touching, and questioning the world around them. Every "why", every messy experiment, and every wide-eyed observation is their way of learning and growing.

Sure, it can be exhausting — and yes, it's often messy — but this innate curiosity is how children discover who they are, how things work, and where they fit in the world. And here's the best part: you get to be their guide on this journey of discovery, encouraging their wonder while keeping your sanity intact.

Together, let's transform those "whys" into opportunities for growth and lifelong learning.

The Psychology of Curiosity

Why are children obsessed with questions like why the sky is blue or what happens when they jump in a puddle? It's because their developing brain thrives on exploration. Curiosity isn't just a personality trait — it's a key driver of cognitive, social, and emotional development.

Children build knowledge through interaction with their environment. They construct "mental maps" (or schemas) to make sense of the world. For example, when a child learns that dogs bark, they might initially think that all animals bark. But when they meet a cow, they adjust their mental map to understand that cows moo instead.

THE FIRST SECRET: CONNECTION

We, as parents, just need to guide and encourage their discoveries, fostering a love for exploration that will last a lifetime.

How to Encourage Curiosity (While Keeping the Joy Alive)

Ready to nurture your little one's spark of wonder? Here's how to turn their endless questions and explorations into meaningful growth:

1. <u>Reframe "No" Into Learning Opportunities</u>- Kids hear "no" a lot, but what if you could channel their curiosity instead of shutting it down? Instead of saying, "Don't touch that", try, "Let's see how it works safely together." This approach shifts the focus from restriction to exploration, giving them a safe way to satisfy their curiosity.
2. <u>Provide Hands-On Experiences</u>- Children learn best by doing, so let them get their hands dirty!

- Sensory Play: Sandboxes, water tables, and playdough are fantastic for tactile exploration.
- Nature Walks: Let them touch leaves, observe bugs, or feel the wind. Bring a magnifying glass to look at details or collect treasures like pinecones.

These hands-on experiences allow children to explore with all their senses, creating deeper, more meaningful connections with their environment.

3. <u>Encourage Open-Ended Play</u>- The best toys aren't the ones with bells and whistles — they're the ones that spark imagination and creativity. Toys like building-blocks, art supplies, dress-up clothes, or even empty cardboard boxes can be transformed into castles, spaceships, or anything else children dream up.

Tip: Open-ended play gives you a much-needed breather and helps them dive into their imaginative world.

4. <u>Ask Questions Instead of Giving Answers</u>- When your children ask, "Why do leaves fall?" resist the urge to jump in with a full explanation. Instead, make it a collaborative exploration. Try to respond with: "What do you think?" or "Let's explore that together."

This approach encourages critical thinking and problem-solving while making the learning process interactive and fun. Bonus: It buys you time to Google the answer if needed!

Real-Life Scenario: Nikhil, the Budding Scientist

Meet Nikhil, a curious four-year-old who loved mixing flour, water, and paint into a gooey mess. At first, his parents were frustrated — until his mom saw it as an opportunity.

She introduced him to safe kitchen ingredients like baking soda and vinegar, turning his messy experiments into mini science projects. Over time, Nikhil's curiosity blossomed into a genuine love for understanding how things work.

Yes, it was messy. Yes, it required patience. But the result? A happy, engaged child — and a parent-child bond strengthened through shared discovery.

Specially for Single or Working Parents: You've Got This!

Curiosity thrives on quality, not quantity. So, make the most of the time you have-

THE FIRST SECRET: CONNECTION

1. Micro-Moments Matter: Use everyday moments, like a walk to the store or a car ride, to ask open-ended questions like "What do you think the clouds look like today?" and spark curiosity.
2. Curiosity on the Go: Keep small items like a magnifying glass, crayons, or a notepad handy for impromptu explorations during errands or downtime.
3. Lean on Resources: Audiobooks, educational videos, or curiosity-themed apps can fuel their love of learning when you can't be hands-on.

A Fun Tool: The "Why Chain"

We've all been there: your child asks, "Why does it rain?" and before you know it, you're trapped in an endless loop of "whys". Here's how to turn it into a game:

- Child: "Why does it rain?"
- Parent: "Why do you think clouds hold water?"

Each "why" builds on the last, encouraging deeper thinking and keeping the conversation engaging.

Bonus: It also gives you time to figure out the answer (or to admit you're stumped)!

When you nurture your children's curiosity, you're doing far more than just answering their questions — you're instilling a mindset. You're teaching them to view the world as a place of endless possibilities, where questions are celebrated, and ideas are tested. This curiosity will serve them far beyond their early years. It will fuel their creativity, strengthen their problem-solving skills, and help them approach life with a sense of wonder.

2.1 THE FOUNDATION YEARS (1 TO 5 YEARS)

Quick Activity: Curiosity in Action

1. Observe and Engage: Watch children for 5 minutes while they play or explore. Write down one question they ask or something they seem fascinated by.
2. Your Turn: Ask them an open-ended question like: "What do you think will happen if we try this?"
3. Let Them Lead: Follow their lead in exploring the question together.
4. Reflect: What did you notice about their curiosity or way of exploring?

This small moment of connection can inspire their love for learning — and remind you of the joy in their endless "whys". Make a bonding notebook, create sections and do the activities in it so that you have a memory bank at the end of the year.

Let's get messy, stay curious, and enjoy the ride. You're raising a thoughtful, imaginative, and brave explorer — and as always, I'm here cheering you on every step of the way!

2.1.3: Play as a Pathway to Growth

For the little one, play is serious business. It's how they learn, grow, and make sense of the world. Whether they're pretending to be astronauts, hosting a tea party for teddy bears, or constructing a block tower, every playful moment is packed with opportunities for development.

In this chapter, we'll explore the profound role of play in children's growth, how to make the most of these moments, and how you can join the fun while fostering essential skills.

THE FIRST SECRET: CONNECTION

Have you heard about the Hygiene Hypothesis?

This will give you a new perspective for sure. Too much cleanliness in early childhood can weaken a child's immune system, leading to allergies, asthma, or autoimmune issues later in life.

- The immune system needs exposure to germs to learn what is harmful and what isn't.
- Over-sanitizing and limited outdoor play reduce contact with helpful microbes, causing the immune system to overreact to harmless things like dust, pollen, or certain foods.

So now dear parents,

1. Let Kids Get Dirty: Allow outdoor play in soil, sand, and nature.
2. Limit Over-Sanitizing: Avoid excessive use of antibacterial products at home.
3. Encourage Pets: Growing up with pets can help strengthen the immune system.
4. Support Gut Health: Include foods like yoghurt, fruits, and veggies for healthy gut bacteria.

Let the children explore, play, and embrace a little dirt. It helps their immune system grow strong and resilient! 🌱

Types of Play and Their Benefits

Different kinds of play offer unique developmental advantages:

1. Imaginative Play: Pretending to be superheroes, running a store, or hosting a tea party fosters creativity, problem-solving, and emotional regulation. So, dressing up as a firefighter and "saving the day" teaches empathy and perseverance.

2.1 THE FOUNDATION YEARS (1 TO 5 YEARS)

2. Physical Play: Activities like running, jumping, or climbing develop coordination, resilience, and physical strength. Playing tag not only burns energy but also hones decision-making as kids strategize to avoid being caught.
3. Social Play: Interacting with peers during group games helps children learn teamwork, communication, and conflict resolution. So, building a fort together requires sharing materials and agreeing on a design — valuable life skills!
4. Exploratory Play: Tinkering with objects, mixing colors, or observing bugs nurtures curiosity, critical thinking, and sensory development. Like feeling sand, pouring water, and stacking rocks on a beach ignites sensory and problem-solving skills.

Foster Growth Through Play

Here's how you can encourage meaningful play experiences while strengthening your bond with children:

1. Prioritize Free Play- Let children take the lead. Whether they're doodling, pretending to be a chef, or creating their own games, free play is their way of exploring the world.
   Pro Tip: Step back and let their imagination unfold but stay nearby to encourage or support them if needed.
   If they're building with blocks and ask you for help, guide them by asking, "What do you think we should try next?"
2. Be an Engaged Play Partner- Join the child's imaginative world! Be a customer in their store, a dragon in their kingdom, or simply an interested observer. For example, if they're "cooking" with toy food, pretend to taste it and say, "Yum! This is the

THE FIRST SECRET: CONNECTION

best pretend pizza I've ever had!" Your enthusiasm shows them their creativity is valued.
3. Choose Open-Ended Toys- The best toys are the ones that grow with children and spark endless possibilities. Blocks, puzzles, art supplies, dolls, dress-up clothes, or even a cardboard box can transform into anything their imagination dreams up.
4. Create Social Play Opportunities- Arrange playdates, head to the park, or join community activities where children can interact with peers. Social play is essential for teaching teamwork, empathy, and communication.

Tip: Resist the urge to micromanage. Let children navigate social dynamics while offering support if they need help sharing or resolving conflicts.

There is a common problem I hear from parents: Hitting... If your child hits other children in the playground, it's essential to address the behaviour calmly and constructively. Here's a step-by-step guide to handle the situation effectively:

Immediate Actions

1. Stay Calm: Avoid reacting with anger or frustration. Staying calm sets the tone for a thoughtful response and prevents escalating the situation.
2. Separate the Children: Gently intervene to stop the behavior. Separate your child from the other child involved to prevent further conflict.
3. Ensure Safety: Check if the other child is hurt and address any injuries immediately. Offer a sincere apology to the other child and their caregiver.

Talk to Your Child

4. Address the Behavior, Not the Child: Use language that focuses on the action, not labeling the child. For example say, "Hitting is not okay," instead of "You're a bad child."
5. Validate Their Feelings: Acknowledge their emotions. For example, "I see that you're upset or frustrated, but hitting is not the way to solve problems."
6. Ask for Their Perspective: Encourage them to explain what happened. This helps you understand the trigger and shows your child that their feelings matter.
7. Teach Empathy: Help your child understand how their actions affect others. For example, "When you hit, it hurts the other person, and they feel sad."

Teach Alternatives

8. Offer Better Ways to Express Emotions: Teach them to use words to express anger or frustration, such as saying, "I don't like that," or seeking help from an adult.
9. Practice Problem-Solving: Role-play scenarios where they might feel frustrated and guide them on how to handle the situation without hitting anyone.
10. Encourage Physical Outlets: Redirect their energy by suggesting positive physical activities like jumping, running, or squeezing a stress ball when they feel overwhelmed.

Follow Up

11. Model Appropriate Behavior: Show how to resolve conflicts peacefully. Your child learns a lot by watching how you handle disagreements.

12. Set Consistent Boundaries: Reinforce that hitting is never acceptable. Be firm yet kind in repeating this rule when necessary.
13. Encourage an Apology: Guide your child to apologize to the other child. Help them use kind words like, "I'm sorry for hitting you. I won't do it again."
14. Praise Positive Behavior: Recognize and praise your child when they handle conflicts appropriately, reinforcing positive actions.

If It's a Recurring Issue

15. Identify Triggers: Observe patterns in their behavior. Is hitting more likely when they're tired, hungry, or overstimulated?
16. Build Emotional Regulation Skills: Teach them techniques like deep breathing or counting to ten to calm down in stressful situations.
17. Seek Professional Help if Needed: If the behavior persists despite consistent guidance, consider consulting a child psychologist or counselor for additional support.

Key Takeaway

Addressing hitting behavior in the playground is an opportunity to teach your child valuable social and emotional skills. By responding calmly, teaching alternatives, and reinforcing empathy, you can guide them toward better ways of interacting with others. Address this during the golden hour, create a story and do a heart-to-heart conversation on this to make an impact in the kids.

2.1 THE FOUNDATION YEARS (1 TO 5 YEARS)

Case Study: Aarav's Pretend Store

Meet Aarav, a five-year-old who spent hours setting up a pretend store with old boxes and cans. His parents could have seen the clutter as a nuisance, but instead, they joined in as customers.

Through play, Aarav learned:

- Math Skills: Adding up prices in his store.
- Communication: Practicing polite phrases like "Thank you for shopping!"
- Decision-Making: Deciding how to set up and manage his store.

By engaging with Aarav's imaginative world, his parents turned a simple activity into a joyful learning experience for everyone.

Quick Activity: Playful Connection

<u>DIY Imagination Box:</u>

Fill a box with random items (spoons, scarves, cardboard) and encourage creative play.

Figure 8

Keep changing the items in the DIY BOX and give it to the child when the child says, "I am bored."

The Bigger Picture

Play isn't just entertainment; it's a gateway to lifelong skills. Through play, children learn to navigate challenges, express emotions, and explore possibilities. It's their classroom, therapy, and happy place rolled into one.

Whether it's pretending to be pirates, exploring the backyard, or building the tallest tower ever, every moment of play is an opportunity for children to grow. And guess what? It's an opportunity for you, too — to laugh, connect, and rediscover the magic of childhood.

Remember, I'm here cheering you on every step of the way. Let's make every playful moment count! ✨

2.1.4: Handling Tantrums – The Porcupine Quill Approach

Let's talk tantrums — a challenge that feels like trying to reason with a tiny, very loud lawyer who isn't fluent in logic yet. Think of tantrums as the emotional equivalent of a porcupine raising its quills. They're not attacks; they're protective reactions to overwhelming emotions children haven't yet learnt to manage.

By understanding what's going on inside children's developing brains and adopting a calm, empathetic approach, you can turn these prickly moments into opportunities for growth, connection, and even a laugh or two.

Understand Child Psychology

Imagine a child's brain as a house under construction. The emotional center (the limbic system) is fully operational — it's the plumbing and wiring of feelings. But the prefrontal cortex, responsible for regulating emotions and solving problems, is still being built. Why do toddlers frequently "flip their lid"? When emotions overwhelm them, tantrums happen — not as defiance, but as a signal that they need help navigating their feelings.

Porcupine Quill Analogy

Let me share this interesting analogy, which I created while watching porcupine on TV. When a porcupine feels threatened, it raises its quills — not to attack, but to protect itself. Similarly, tantrums are a child's way of saying, "I' don't know what's happening to me!" Meeting these "quills" with anger only escalates the situation. Instead, respond with patience and empathy to help children feel safe enough to "lower their quills."

Understanding the Causes of Tantrums

Tantrums are often triggered by unmet needs or developmental hurdles:

- Physical Needs: Hunger, fatigue, or overstimulation (junk food, high sugar or salt)
- Emotional Overload: Big feelings they can't yet manage.
- Developmental Stage: Limited language for expressing their complex emotions.
- Seeking Attention: A sign that emotional needs aren't being met.

THE FIRST SECRET: CONNECTION

- Testing Boundaries: Exploring limits and learning what's acceptable.
- Excessive Screens: No boundaries on screen time.

Ten Strategies for Managing Tantrums

Figure 9

1. Stay Calm and Compose: Your energy sets the tone. A calm parent helps soothe an upset child. Take deep breaths, count to ten, or visualize a calm beach before responding.
2. Recognize Triggers
   Observe patterns to identify situations that may lead to tantrums. Are they more likely after a loud outing, during a change in routine, or when your child feels overwhelmed? Recognizing these triggers allows you to address the root causes proactively.
3. Proactive Strategies
   Use visual schedules to help children anticipate changes. Offer choices to give them a sense of control. Maintain

structured routines to reduce feelings of unpredictability and frustration.

4. Co-Regulation Techniques
   Empathy First: Validate their feelings by acknowledging them. For example, "I see you're upset because it's so loud. Let's find a quieter spot together."
   Calm Cues: Provide tools for self-soothing, like noise-cancelling headphones, fidget toys, or a weighted blanket.

5. Label and Validate Emotions
   Help your children identify and understand their feelings. For instance, "You're upset because we have to leave the park. It's okay to feel upset." This builds emotional awareness and vocabulary.

6. Create a Safe Space
   Offer a non-judgmental environment for your children to reset. Reassure them with statements like, "I'm here if you need me. Take your time to calm down."

7. Use Simple, Clear Communication
   Keep instructions concise and easy to understand. For example, "Let's breathe together" or "I'm here to help." Overwhelmed children may struggle with processing complex directions.

8. Introduce Calming Techniques
   Practice deep breathing: Inhale through the nose, hold for three seconds, and exhale slowly. Use a glitter jar: Shake it and watch the glitter settle to symbolize calming emotions. Employ physical touch: A gentle hug or touch can release oxytocin, helping reduce stress for both parent and child.

9. Offer Distractions

THE FIRST SECRET: CONNECTION

Redirect attention to interrupt the tantrum cycle. Suggest activities like drawing, telling a calming story, or giving them a favorite toy.

10. Set Boundaries Calmly
    Validate emotions while guiding behavior. For example, "It's okay to feel angry, but it's not okay to hit. Let's find another way to show how you feel."

By implementing these strategies, you create a supportive framework for managing tantrums while helping children develop emotional resilience and self-regulation skills.

Pro tip: Be consistent in these strategies – children may not listen to you many times, and they will test your boundaries, but you need to keep yourself calm and be consistent. Only then will the child understand. When children throw tantrums, their logical brain is not working so they cannot understand you.

Turning Tantrums into Learning Opportunities

When approached with empathy, tantrums can become teachable moments.

1. Post-Tantrum Reflection- What to Say: "Next time you feel upset, let's talk about it so I can help."
2. Reinforce Positive Behavior- What to Say: "I'm proud of you for using your words instead of yelling."
3. It also teaches the kids to label their emotions and gradually learn to manage them.

Remember: Every time you respond with patience, you're teaching children essential self-regulation skills.

Quick Activity: Trigger Tracker: Decode and Respond

Create a Table and write it down. Use it every day.

1. Trigger: What caused the tantrum?
2. Behavior: How did your child react?
3. Your Reaction: How did you handle it?
4. Plan: What will you do differently next time?
5. Outcome: What worked?

Use the same bonding notebook to maintain this tracker as well. You can also make an excel sheet- take a printout and stick it on the fridge with a pen or marker to fill it.

Parenting isn't about avoiding tantrums — it's about navigating them with grace. You're doing an incredible job, and every empathetic response strengthens the bond with your children while teaching them lifelong skills.

2.1.5: Feeding with Love and Surviving Mealtime Battles

Feeding your little one is a special kind of adventure — equal parts nurturing, bonding and (let's be honest) chaos. From those dreamy early days of breastfeeding or bottle-feeding to the full-blown negotiations over broccoli, feeding children is a rollercoaster ride of love, mess, and maybe a few tears (yours and theirs).

This chapter is here to help you feed children with confidence, joy, and maybe even a little laughter.

Feeding your baby is one of the first ways you connect and care for them. However, the transition from the milk feed to solids can be quite a challenge. In this chapter, we'll explore why children can develop peculiar attitudes toward food and how to make mealtimes stress-free. The food habits we establish during our children's early years often become lifelong patterns.

When I had my first child, I didn't know — and no one really told me — that children don't need salt or sugar until the age of two. I learned this from our pediatrician. There were many similar things I discovered along the way.

Why Toddlers Are So Weird About Food

1. Power Moves: Your toddler's refusal to eat those green beans? It's not about the beans. It's about proving they're the boss of their plate.
2. Food Fears: New foods are *suspicious*. What is that broccoli plotting, anyway?
3. Super-Tasters in Training: Toddlers' taste buds are extra sensitive, so those mild peppers you love might feel like fire to them.

Children between the ages of 1 and 5 have approximately 10,000 taste buds, significantly more than adults. These taste buds are distributed not only on their tongues but also on the sides, roof, and back of their mouths. Repeated exposure (up to 10–15 times) to a new food can help children accept and enjoy it, even if they initially reject it.

Making Mealtime Stress-Free with 10 Strategies

Mealtime doesn't have to be a battle. With a little preparation and a lot of patience, you can turn it into a fun and meaningful experience for you and your children.

2.1 THE FOUNDATION YEARS (1 TO 5 YEARS)

1. Keep It Chill- Stick to a consistent mealtime routine, such as dinner at 6 PM at the table. But don't stress if children skip a meal — they'll make up for it when they're hungry.
2. Finger foods are winners- finger foods like parantha rolls can be filled with various nutritious stuffings such as paneer, potato, spinach, corn, beetroot, and more. These not only provide essential nutrients but also keep kids happy and engaged during meals.
3. Play with Food- Make mealtime enjoyable by involving children. Let them help with simple cooking tasks as they become Mini Chefs or play games like the "Taste Test Challenge" to explore new foods. Detailed instructions for these activities are provided at the end.
4. Respect Their Appetites- Forget the old "clean plate club." Serve small portions and allow children to ask for seconds. Respect their hunger cues instead of forcing them to finish everything.
5. Celebrate Wins (Even Tiny Ones)- Did they try one bite of broccoli? Celebrate it! Every small step counts. Offer praise without pressuring them and keep introducing new foods.
6. Explore Food Together- Take children for vegetable shopping. Let them touch, feel, and talk about different vegetables. This involvement sparks curiosity and openness to trying new things.
7. Balancing the Feeding Act- Feeding doesn't have to be all-or-nothing:
   - Weaning Wisely: Transition to solids at your baby's pace. No rush, no guilt.

8. Fun Tips for Sanity at Mealtime
   - Mood Tracker: Note what's served, your children's reactions, and any patterns that emerge.
   - Keep It Light: Ask fun questions like, "What does this taste like to you?" to make meals interactive.
9. Let Hunger Lead: Skip chasing your toddler with a spoon. When they're hungry, they'll eat — and it works! This helps them understand the importance of food. Stay consistent, and resist the urge to give in, even when it's tough.
10. Limit Junk Food Consumption – While occasional treats are fine, prioritise a healthy lifestyle by choosing nutritious options. Early exposure to healthy foods helps develop good eating habits. Remember, the word "junk" is right there in "junk food."

Did you know Junk Food affects the Nervous System?

Children's developing bodies and brains are highly sensitive to junk food.

Junk food has a Multiplier Effect on kids:

- 1 packet of chips for kids = 3 packets for adults, 1 chocolate for kids = 5 chocolates for adults.

Due to their smaller size, kids experience a more intense effect from unhealthy fats, sugar, and additives.

Some immediate effects which we notice in our kids -

1. Sugar Rush: Overloads the brain, causing hyperactivity and mood swings.
2. Crash: Sharp drops in blood sugar led to fatigue and irritability.

2.1 THE FOUNDATION YEARS (1 TO 5 YEARS)

3. Nervous Overdrive: The underdeveloped nervous system struggles, causing erratic behavior.

Some more effects which we fail to notice immediately but there are long-term negative effects -

- Weakens the immune system.
- Increases risk of obesity and metabolic issues.
- Affects memory, learning, and brain development.

So, what do you do, dear parents? Follow farm to plate or farm to cook to plate.

- Replace processed snacks with fruits, nuts, or yoghurt.
- Prioritize balanced meals and hydration.
- Teach kids moderation with occasional treats.

Junk food may seem harmless, but its impact on kids is far greater than on adults. Small changes can make a big difference!

Research shows that when children from India, Japan, America, and Britain were asked about their favorite foods, kids from all countries except Japan listed junk food. Japanese children, however, named vegetables as their favorites. This difference stems from the early introduction of healthy foods in their diets. Children often mimic what they see rather than what they're told, so modelling healthy eating habits is key to influencing their choices.

<u>Remember: No Screens During Meals</u>: Screens during meals distract kids, breaking their connection with food.

- Awareness: Kids may not realize what or how much they're eating.

THE FIRST SECRET: CONNECTION

- Brain-Food Link: Seeing and tasting food helps build memory and positive associations.
- Hunger Cues: Screens block natural signals of hunger and fullness.

Create screen-free meals to foster mindful eating and family bonding.

Case Study: The Broccoli Breakthrough

Meet Anaya, a three-year-old who treated vegetables like sworn enemies. Her parents took a new approach:

1. Let her "help" wash and chop veggies in the kitchen.
2. Stayed neutral during meals — no "Eat your veggies!" nagging.
3. Celebrated small wins, like when she nibbled on a carrot.

Fast forward a few months, and Anaya now happily eats broccoli. Who knew patience could taste so good?

Quick Activity: Taste Test Game

Figure 10

- **What You'll Need:** A few bite-sized foods (e.g., apple, cucumber, cheese).
- **How to Play:** Blindfold children (or have them close their eyes) and give them a small bite of food. Let them guess what it is and describe the taste or texture.
- **Why It Works:** This fun game makes trying new foods exciting and pressure-free. Who knows? They might surprise you by loving something new!

I do this activity with my kids when they don't like the food cooked at home or I want them to try something new. Keep changing the items by the way.

One bite at a time, you're building their relationship with food — and with you.

The Bigger Picture

Feeding isn't just about food — it's about connection, learning, and a whole lot of love. Whether you're figuring out breastfeeding, mixing formula bottles, or refereeing dinnertime debates, remember: You're doing an amazing job.

Your little one doesn't need perfect meals — they need a parent who shows up, loves them, and makes mealtimes a space for joy (and maybe a little silliness).

2.1.6: Sleep Challenges and Routines – Creating Restful Nights

Let's talk about sleep — children's secret weapon for growth and your ticket to sanity. It's the magical time when little bodies and minds recharge but getting there can sometimes feel like a marathon of bedtime stalling, monster fears, and sleep regressions.

Don't worry — you're not alone. This chapter is here to help you navigate common sleep challenges and craft a peaceful bedtime routine that works for your family. Let's turn bedtime battles into sweet dreams!

Why Sleep is a Big Deal

Sleep isn't just about rest — it's when the magic happens:
- Brain Development: Sleep helps children's brain consolidate learning and build neural connections.
- Emotional Regulation: A well-rested child is better equipped to handle big feelings and frustration.
- Physical Growth: Deep sleep triggers the release of growth hormones, fueling healthy development.

Understanding the Psychology of Sleep

1. Attachment and Sleep - It is a secure bond with you that helps children feel safe and ready to drift off to sleep peacefully. As per the psychologists, we should actually co-sleep with the kids till the age of 5 as kids get that warmth and energy from their parents. Research says kids who sleep with their parents are emotionally strong and do bed-wetting much less than the others. It helps in reducing stress for both parent and child.
2. The Golden Hour- The hour before sleep is prime time for positive rituals. Calm affirmations or soothing routines during this period can leave a lasting impression on children's subconscious.

3. Circadian Rhythms- Children's internal clocks thrive on consistency. Aligning routines with these rhythms makes bedtime smoother and mornings brighter.

Common Sleep Challenges and Solutions

1. Bedtime Resistance: Toddlers love asserting independence — and bedtime is prime territory for power struggles.
    - *Offer choices: "Do you want the blue pajamas or the yellow ones?"*
    - *Use cues: Dim lights and play calming music 30 minutes before bed.*
    - *Introduce a Bedtime Pass: Give children one "pass" for a final hug or drink to minimize stalling.*

2. Nighttime Fears: Their growing imagination can turn harmless shadows into scary monsters.
    - *Validate: "I know the dark feels scary, but you're safe, and I'm here."*
    - *Use comforting tools: Try a "monster spray" (water in a fun spray bottle) or a favorite stuffed animal as their nighttime protector.*

3. Sleep Regressions: Developmental milestones like walking or talking can disrupt sleep temporarily.
    - *Stick to routines even during rough patches.*
    - *Reassure without creating new habits you don't want long-term (e.g., sleeping in their bed).*

THE FIRST SECRET: CONNECTION

Crafting a Calming Bedtime Routine

A predictable bedtime routine helps ease the transition from playtime to sleep. What you allow prevails!

Example Routine

1. Warm Bath: A soothing way to signal bedtime.
2. Storytime: Pick a calming book or life skills book to share together.
3. Affirmations: End with a positive statement like, "You are safe and loved."
4. Lights Out: Use dim lighting or a soft nightlight for a serene atmosphere.

Golden Hour Tips

- Avoid screens before bed to prevent melatonin disruption.
- Engage in quiet bonding activities like reading, singing, or sharing cuddles.
- Positive Affirmations
- Listen to the child
- Gratitude Prayer is a must
- The brain goes into theta mode, so their 'yes' brain is activated. Use this time to teach them essential life lessons.

Innovative Tools for Better Sleep

1. The Sleep Basket: Fill a basket with bedtime essentials like a favorite blanket, book, or stuffed animal. This signals consistency and comfort.

2. Dream Jars: Decorate a jar together and fill it with "dream tickets" featuring sweet ideas like "floating on clouds" or "playing with puppies."
3. Glow Path: Use battery-operated lights to create a glowing path to the bathroom or your room, easing fears of the dark.

Case Study: Aarav's Bedtime Success

Four-year-old Aarav dreaded bedtime, turning it into a nightly negotiation. His parents tried a new approach:

- Introduced a visual timer to signal when bedtime started.
- Crafted a routine that included his favorite book and affirmations like, "Tomorrow will be a great day."
- Used a Bedtime Pass to give him control over one final request.

Within two weeks, bedtime went from chaos to calm, and Aarav happily settled into his nightly routine.

Flexibility Within Structure

Life happens! Here's how to maintain balance:

- Special Occasions: Allow occasional deviations (holidays or vacations) but return to routines quickly.
- Rebuilding Routines: Shift bedtime gradually in 15-minute increments if needed to get back on track.

This is for You, Parents...

After your kids fall asleep tonight, take five minutes to jot down one moment that went well. For example, "They smiled after I sang their favorite lullaby."

THE FIRST SECRET: CONNECTION

Pro Tip: Do these 3 to 5 times alone or with your partner.
- *"Smell the flowers"* 🌼 *(inhale deeply through the nose).*
- *"Blow out the candles"* 🕯 *(exhale slowly through the mouth).*

These small rituals can rejuvenate you and create positive memories in your brain.

Activity: Bedtime Visual Chart
Step-by-Step Routine

GOLDEN HOUR BEDTIME CHECKLIST
@parenting_swati
- ☐ Change to Night Dress
- ☐ Brush Teeth + Use Washroom
- ☐ Read a Book
- ☐ Pillow Talk with Parents
- ☐ GratitudePrayer + Affirmation

Figure 11

Use pictures to represent each task:
- *Putting on pajamas* 👕
- *Brushing teeth* 🪥
- *Reading a story on life skills or moral stories* 📖
- *Pillow talk* 🌙
- *Turning off the light* 💡

Place it where children can see and follow it daily. Do it for 21 days consistently to form a habit and for 66 days to form a lifestyle.

The Bigger Picture

Sleep isn't just about rest — it's about growth, connection, and peace for your whole family. Challenges like bedtime resistance or nighttime fears are opportunities to strengthen your bond and teach children the value of rest.

Rest easy, parents — you're creating more than a sleep routine. You're building a foundation of love and security that will carry children through life. 🌙✨

2.1.7: Managing Screen Time in the Digital Age – Finding Balance

Screens are everywhere — tiny hands tapping on tablets, eyes glued to cartoons, and pleas of "just five more minutes!" Managing screen time in today's world can feel overwhelming, but don't worry. This chapter is here to help you find balance, set boundaries, and use screens in ways that support children's growth while keeping real-world connections alive.

Why Screens Are So Alluring?

Screens are like magnets for little ones because:
- Brain Stimulation: Bright colors, catchy sounds, and fast-moving images release dopamine, making screens highly engaging.
- Self-Regulation Struggles: Kids don't yet have the skills to stop themselves, so transitions away from screens can be tough.

The Risks of Too Much Screen Time

While screens can be educational, overuse has downsides:

THE FIRST SECRET: CONNECTION

- Language Delays: Screens can replace crucial face-to-face interactions needed for language development.
- Emotional Overload: Overstimulation can make managing boredom or frustration harder.
- Reduced Physical Activity: Time on screens means less time for active play and motor skill development.

Healthy Screen Time Guidelines

Based on The American Academy of Pediatrics recommendations:
- 0–18 Months: No screens (except video chats).
- 18–24 Months: High-quality content with parental guidance.
- 2–5 Years: Up to 1 hour/day of educational content.
- 6–10 Years: 1–2 hours/day, balanced with active play and learning.
- 11–18 Years: Self-regulated use, emphasizing balance and online safety.

Pro Tips

- Avoid screens during meals or an hour before bed.
- Keep bedrooms screen-free zones.
- Create a family screentime rule. For example, in my house screens are only allowed on Fridays and Saturdays (for my elder one there is a limit of 1 hour and for my younger one the limit is 30 minutes).

The Psychology of Screen Time Management - 10 Strategies

1. Choose Quality Content - Select programs that encourage creativity, problem-solving, or language development.

2.1 THE FOUNDATION YEARS (1 TO 5 YEARS)

Intentional use of educational and interactive content can spark imagination and learning.
2. Co-view and Engage- Watch content together and connect it to real-life experiences. For example, after watching a nature show, go on a walk and spot similar animals or plants. Engage your child by asking questions like, "What do you think happens next?" to encourage critical thinking.
3. Balance Screens with Active Play - For every 20 minutes of screen time, ensure children have time for physical activity, imaginative play, or exploration. Follow the 20-20-20 Rule: Every 20 minutes, look at something 20 feet away for 20 seconds to reduce eye strain.
4. Structured Routines - Set clear expectations for when and how much screen time is allowed. For instance, "You can have screen time after breakfast for 20 minutes." Predictable schedules help children understand boundaries and reduce resistance.
5. Use Visual Timers - Countdown clocks or sand timers can help children transition away from screens. Provide a five-minute reminder before screen time ends to prepare them for the change.
6. Offer Engaging Alternatives - Redirect their attention with fun and interactive options like drawing, playing with blocks, or outdoor activities. For example, "Screen time is over — let's draw a picture!"
7. Model Healthy Habits - Children mimic what they see. Avoid excessive screen use during family time and establish screen-free zones like the dining table and bedrooms to promote real-world interactions and better sleep hygiene.

THE FIRST SECRET: CONNECTION

8. Acknowledge Feelings and Offer Support - Transitions can be difficult. Empathize with children by saying, "I know it's hard to stop. Let's take a deep breath and find something fun to do next."

Figure 12

9. Create Screen-Free Zones- Designate areas like the dining room or bedrooms as screen-free spaces. This encourages face-to-face communication and supports healthy routines like undisturbed family meals or bedtime rituals.
10. Create Screen-free rewards- No screens for a day can give the child 30 minutes of free play or outdoor play. The reward system motivates my little one a lot and he is ready to miss his weekend screens as well.

By combining active engagement, structured routines, and empathetic strategies, screen time becomes not just a source of entertainment but a tool for learning, bonding, and creativity. So, it's important to follow the 4P Rule for screen management:

1. Purpose: Is it for learning, bonding, or relaxation?
2. Program: Is the content age-appropriate and enriching?

2.1 THE FOUNDATION YEARS (1 TO 5 YEARS)

3. Presence: Are you engaging with children during or after screen time?
4. Proportion: Is screen time balanced with other activities like play and rest?

Use this simple guide to evaluate screen time of the child. Make a sheet of it daily.

Case Study: Aarushi's Screen Time Reset

Three-year-old Aarushi loved her tablet but often melted down when it was time to stop. Her parents tried this:

- Countdown Timers: A visual timer helped her prepare for transitions.
- Engaging Alternatives: They offered her coloring books and puzzles after screen time.
- Evening Routine: Screens were swapped for bedtime stories and cuddles.

Within weeks, Aarushi adapted, and family time became more enjoyable.

Quick Activity: Your Family's Screen Rules

Screen-Free Reward Jar or Chart
1. How It Works:
    - *Add a token to the jar for every 30 minutes (or set duration) of screen-free time.*
2. Exciting Rewards: Tokens can be exchanged for fun rewards like:
    - *A story-time session* 📖
    - *A special snack* 🍪

THE FIRST SECRET: CONNECTION

- *A family game night* 🎲
- *Extra playtime outside* 🌳

Encourage positive habits while making it fun and rewarding! Honestly, who doesn't like rewards? There is an element of surprise and something to look forward to.

The Bigger Picture

Screens are a part of modern life, but with intentionality and balance, they can be tools rather than distractions. Some days will have more screen time than others — and that's okay. What matters is your effort to create healthy habits and meaningful connections, on-screen and off.

You've got this, parents! ✨

2.1.8: Navigating Milestones and Developmental Concerns – Embracing Every Step

Milestones are magical — those first steps, first words, and first giggles are moments you'll treasure forever. But let's be honest: milestones can also spark stress. The endless questions creep in: "Why isn't my child walking yet?", "Should they know their colors by now?"

Here's the truth: milestones are guides, not grades. Every child grows at their own pace, charting a path as unique as they are. Let's embrace the quirks, celebrate the progress, and handle developmental concerns with grace and humor.

2.1 THE FOUNDATION YEARS (1 TO 5 YEARS)

The Psychology of Milestones

1. Milestones offer a sense of security, like signposts that everything is on track.
2. Social media and playground chatter can turn milestones into a competition, but every child's timeline is different.

Growth happens when kids are gently supported in tasks just beyond their current abilities. It's about encouragement, not speed.

Let us celebrate how far our children have come. Simple things like "Last month, she couldn't hold a crayon. Now she's drawing squiggly masterpieces!" Some children master language first, others excel in motor skills. Both paths are normal.

Every "first" — no matter how small — deserves a celebration. Did they wave for the first time? Did they stack two blocks? Shower them with smiles and cheers! These moments build confidence and remind you to savor the journey.

Understanding Natural Variations in Growth

1. Speech Delays: Some kids are busy exploring movement before words. Boys, in particular, may have slight speech delays. Many kids are suffering from speech delays because of high screen time, especially by watching highly stimulating videos like cartoons.
2. Motor Skills: Some kids observe before diving in. Early walkers don't always become Olympians — it's all about their individual comfort zone.

In milestones, a common thing parents compare is: potty training. Is your child potty trained? It is a huge question and answering it

THE FIRST SECRET: CONNECTION

comes with the pressure of judgement. Let me share my journey with you.

Potty Training: A Tale of My Two Kids

Potty training is one of those parenting milestones that leaves you with plenty of stories — and maybe a few laughs in hindsight. For my daughter, it was a breeze. She hated the idea of dirty diapers so much that she wouldn't even let one get messy. Before long, she was running to the potty like a pro.

But then came my son, oh boy, it was a journey! He loved the fresh feel of a clean diaper... so much so that he'd wait until I changed him before making it dirty again. Every single time. Let's just say patience wasn't just a virtue; it was a survival strategy.

Every child is different, but here are a few signs:

- Staying dry for longer periods.
- Showing discomfort with wet diapers — or little one's case, insisting on soiling only fresh ones!
- Following you into the bathroom with an air of curiosity, like she did, shadowing my every move.

What Worked for Us
1. Make It Fun: Potty time is celebration time! Stickers, reward charts, and plenty of cheers turned it into a game she loved. For my son, potty-themed books were a game-changer.
2. Stay Patient: Accidents happen, and they're all part of learning. Deep breaths are your best friend.

3. Build a Routine: Regular trips to the potty — after meals, naps, or playtime — helped set the habit. It also saved a lot of diapers!
4. Celebrate the Wins: Even the smallest victories deserve a round of applause. A simple "I'm so proud of you!" works wonders.
5. Let Them Lead: It's not a race. Some days will feel like breakthroughs; others, not so much. That's okay.

Potty training is a messy, funny, sometimes frustrating milestone, but it's one worth celebrating. Whether it's smooth sailing like her journey or a wild ride like his, every tiny success is a step forward. You're doing amazing — and so are they. Keep going; you've got this!

When to Seek Professional Guidance

Trust your gut. If something feels off, don't hesitate to check in with a professional. Early support can make all the difference. You can talk to your pediatrician.

Age-Wise Milestone Chart

Age Range	Physical	Cognitive	Language	Social/Emotional
0-6 Months	Lifts head, rolls over, starts sitting with support	Follows objects, shows curiosity about sights and sounds	Coos, gurgles, responds to voices, smiles socially	Smiles socially, enjoys being cuddled, develops attachment
6-12 Months	Sits without support, crawls, stands holding furniture	Explores objects, recognizes familiar faces and objects	Babbles, responds to name, understands 'no' or 'bye-bye'	Separation anxiety, enjoys peek-a-boo, shows emotions
12-18 Months	Walks independently, climbs stairs with help, stacks blocks	Points to objects, imitates gestures, understands object use	Says 10-15 words, follows instructions, points to body parts	Prefers familiar people, enjoys pretend play, asserts independence
18-24 Months	Runs steadily, kicks ball, climbs onto furniture	Matches shapes, begins solving problems, explores curiosity	Says 20-50 words, combines words into short phrases	Imitates others, shows affection, experiences tantrums
2-3 Years	Jumps, climbs stairs, begins pedaling tricycle	Matches shapes/colors, starts understanding numbers	Speaks short sentences, asks 'what' and 'why' questions	Plays alongside others, shares emotions, learns to share
3-4 Years	Hops on one foot, walks stairs alternating feet, draws shapes	Recognizes numbers/letters, follows simple rules	Tells stories, speaks in clear 4-6 word sentences	Plays cooperatively, enjoys dress-up, understands 'mine/yours'
4-5 Years	Skips, throws and catches ball, cuts with scissors	Counts to 10, understands time concepts, follows multi-step instructions	Speaks in full sentences, tells jokes, retells stories	Shows empathy, follows rules, dresses independently

THE FIRST SECRET: CONNECTION

Red Flags to Watch For:

- Speech: No babbling for 12 months or no single words for 18 months.
- Motor Skills: Not sitting for 9 months or walking for 18 months.
- Social Interaction: Avoiding eye contact or not responding to their name.

Easing Milestone Anxiety

1. Development Diary: Keep a journal of children's achievements — big or small. It helps you focus on their progress instead of comparisons.
2. Double Celebrations: Celebrate two milestones at once: "First steps and first high-five — double the joy!"
3. Laugh About the Quirks: One day, you'll cherish the funny mispronunciations and insistence on wearing superhero capes everywhere.

Case Study: The Late Talker Who Became a Storyteller

Rohan's parents were worried when he barely spoke at age two. A speech therapist reassured them he was quietly absorbing language. By age five, Rohan was spinning elaborate tales about pirates and space adventures.

Milestones are less about *when* they happen and more about the love and support you provide along the way.

2.1 THE FOUNDATION YEARS (1 TO 5 YEARS)

Quick Activity: Children's Growth Snapshot

1. Reflect: Write down three milestones your children have reached recently, big or small.
2. Celebrate: Plan one fun way to celebrate their progress this week. Maybe it's a dance party, or a hot chocolate date with children. It's like the Growth celebration.

The Bigger Picture

Parenting isn't a race; and childhood isn't a competition. Milestones are moments to guide you, not to grade you. Celebrate every step, trust your instincts, and embrace the quirks that make children one of a kind.

You're doing an amazing job, and so is your little one. Keep cheering each other on — every step of the way! ✨

2.1.9: Balancing Boundaries - The Art of Guiding Tiny Adventures

Parenting toddlers is like trying to herd cats while they're in a sugar rush — it's equal parts thrilling, chaotic, and full of "how-did-this-happen" moments. Striking the balance between setting boundaries and encouraging their endless curiosity is your secret weapon to raising happy, confident kids.

Think of boundaries as the sturdy frame of a painting and freedom as the bold, messy colors. Together, they create the masterpiece of children's growth and independence.

Why Boundaries and Freedom Matter??

Boundaries: The Safety Net

THE FIRST SECRET: CONNECTION

Boundaries aren't about control; they're about creating a world where children feel safe enough to explore. Consistent rules help kids know what to expect. Learning that actions have consequences builds decision-making skills; otherwise, the brain goes into FIGHT and FLIGHT Mode. So, for the brain to grow properly they need routine.

Exploration is your toddler's full-time job, and their confidence grows with every new discovery.

- Independence: Freedom to explore helps them develop problem-solving skills.
- Growth: Interacting with their environment fuels curiosity and resilience.

Setting Healthy Boundaries

Boundaries work best when they're clear, consistent, and delivered with a sprinkle of empathy.

Keep It Simple
- Instead of "Behave!" try: "We use quiet voices in the library."
- Make rules clear and specific to avoid confusion.

Stick to Your Word
- If bedtime is 7:30 PM, keep it consistent (most nights, at least!).

Empathy Works Wonders
- Acknowledge their feelings while staying firm:
    - *"I know leaving the park is tough, but it's time for dinner."*

2.1 THE FOUNDATION YEARS (1 TO 5 YEARS)

Encouraging Exploration (Without the Chaos)

1. Create a Yes Space: Set up an area where they can explore without hearing "no."
2. Mark Boundaries: Use rugs, tape, or furniture to define safe play zones.
3. Redirect, Don't Deny: Instead of "Don't touch that!" Try: "Here's something fun to play with instead."

Positive Discipline Techniques

Discipline isn't about punishing — it's about teaching.

1. Redirection: "Blocks are for stacking, not throwing. Let's build something cool together."
2. Natural Consequences: "You didn't wear your coat, so now you feel cold. Next time, let's bring it."
3. Logical Consequences: "Juice spilled? Let's grab a towel and clean it up together."
4. Positive Reinforcement: "Thank you for putting your shoes by the door. Great job!"

Balancing Autonomy and Guidance

Encourage independence by giving choices within limits.

- Offer Simple Choices: "Red cup or blue cup?"
- Be Flexible: Bend rules when it makes sense — extra screen time for an educational show is okay.
- Foster Problem-Solving: "What can we do to make cleaning up toys easier?"

THE FIRST SECRET: CONNECTION

A Fun Example: Arjun's Jumping Adventures

Three-year-old Arjun loved jumping on the couch. His parents:
- Created a jumping zone with cushions and a mini trampoline.
- Redirected with consistency: "The couch isn't for jumping, but your trampoline is ready!"

Arjun followed the rule while still enjoying his favorite activity.

Fun Time

1. "I said no snacks on the couch. Now he's eating cookies on the floor. Progress?"
2. "The rule was no drawing on walls. Guess who's now doodling masterpieces on the table?"

Quick Activity: Reflect and Adjust Your Boundaries

1. Observe: What's one boundary you find hard to enforce?
2. Adjust: Can you make it clearer or more consistent?
3. Celebrate: Think of a moment when children respected a rule. How did it feel?

Do the changes and create a mutual schedule with those changes.

The Bigger Picture

Balancing boundaries and freedom is like a dance - not always graceful, but always rewarding. Boundaries keep children safe and secure, while freedom lets them grow into their own confident selves.

Take a deep breath, laugh at the missteps, and remember: you're shaping a kind, curious, and capable little human. That's a win worth celebrating every single day!

2.1.10: Celebrating the Foundation Years

The foundation years — a beautiful, messy, transformative chapter of discovery and growth for both children and you. From first steps to first words (and countless laughs, spills, and hugs in between), these years are filled with moments that shape not only children's future but also your journey as a parent.

As we close this chapter, let's pause to reflect, celebrate, and carry forward the lessons and memories that make these early years so magical.

Cherishing the Small Moments

Parenting is rarely about the big milestones — it's the tiny, everyday moments that fill your heart and home.

Why Small Moments Matter

1. A Mosaic of Memories: It's the belly laughs, bedtime cuddles, and unexpected hugs that stick with you.
2. Strengthening Bonds: Each shared smile and silly game builds love and trust.
3. Embracing Imperfection: The spills, tantrums, and giggles all weave together into the fabric of parenthood.

Guided Reflection

Take a moment to think about:

- The first time they called you "mama" or "papa."
- A challenge that tested your patience but taught you resilience.
- A moment when their laughter turned your day around.

THE FIRST SECRET: CONNECTION

Foundation Years Shape Your Bond

These years are more than just developmental milestones — they're the foundation for a lifelong connection.

As per the Psychology of Bonding, a secure attachment creates trust and emotional resilience. Your love and patience model empathy and connection for children and act like Mirror Neurons. The values you've instilled — curiosity, kindness, and courage — will echo in their actions and choices for years to come.

Lessons Learned Along the Way

Parenting during the foundation years is as much about your growth as it is about theirs.

What You've Taught Children??

- Unconditional Love: They know they're loved, no matter what.
- Resilience: They've learned to get back up after every stumble.
- Curiosity: They've discovered the joy of exploring the world.

What Have Your Children Taught You??

- Fresh Perspective: You've learned to see the world through their wonder-filled eyes.
- The Power of Presence: Little moments mean everything.
- Humor in Chaos: Sometimes, the only thing to do is laugh.

Looking Ahead

As these foundation years come to an end, new adventures await. Children will keep growing, and so will you.

Carry Forward These Lessons

- Lead with Love: The bond you've built is your anchor.
- Celebrate Progress: Every small step forward is worth acknowledging.
- Trust the Journey: You've navigated these years beautifully — what's ahead will unfold in its own perfect way.

10 Checks for Smart Parenting

Go ahead and use these to make your life a little smoother:

1. The Golden Hour- Bedtime Magic: Use consistent routines and calming rituals for restful nights.
2. Hygiene Hypothesis: Let them play in the mud and explore
3. Porcupine Quills = Tantrums: Not meant to hurt you; but your children don't know how to control it either.
4. The Yes Space: Create safe areas for exploration without constant "no's."
5. Co-sleeping: Co-sleeping with your child is a powerful energy explosion tool.
6. Junk Food: Junk food affects the nervous system and creates a multiplier effect in the brain.
7. Taste-Test Fun: Turn mealtimes into playful, pressure-free experiences.
8. Popcorn Brain: Screen time stimulates the child's brain with change of graphics every second.
9. Hug It Out: Remember the 4-8-12 hug rule — 4 hugs a day for survival, 8 for maintenance, 12 for growth.
10. Boundary setting is a boon, not a bane it gives direction and growth.

THE FIRST SECRET: CONNECTION

Planting Seeds of Resilience and Joy

Every small act of love — a bedtime story, a high-five, or a shared moment of wonder — plants seeds of confidence and happiness in children. These seeds will grow into strengths they'll carry with them for life, rooted in the deep, unconditional love you've given them.

A Memory Jar: Quick Reflection Activity

1. Grab a jar and some small slips of paper.
2. Write down one special moment from the foundation years — a laugh, a first word, or a challenge you overcame.
3. Add a new memory each week.

Over time, this jar will become a treasure trove of moments to remind you how magical this journey has been.

The foundation years are building a bond, creating a sense of security, and fostering a love that will last a lifetime with the child. As the child takes their next steps into the world, remember the foundation you've built will carry them forward. You're raising a kind, confident, and curious human being, and the best is yet to come.

Take a deep breath, hug your little one tight, and celebrate how far you've both come. The adventure is just beginning, and it's going to be amazing. ♡

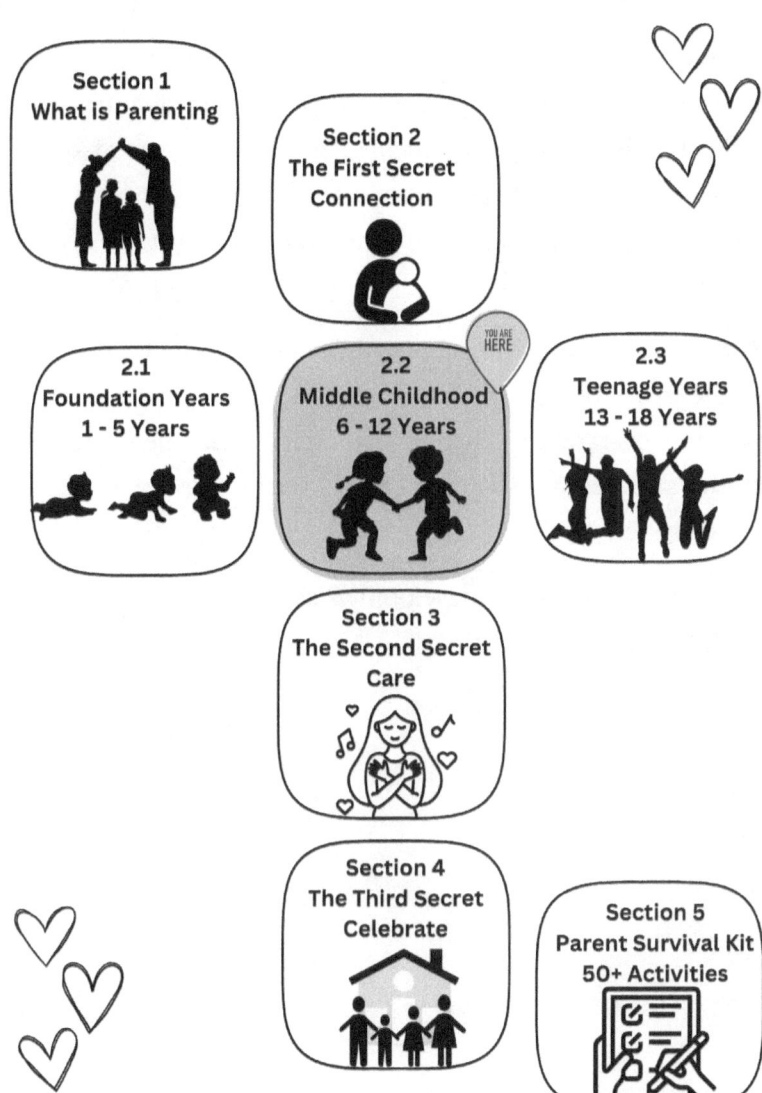

Your Parenting Journey

2.2 Middle Childhood Years: The Growth Stage (6 to 12 Years)

The transition from the foundation years to middle childhood is like watching children step into a whole new world. Your curious toddler is now an energetic, independent school-age child — eager to learn, explore, and test boundaries. With this growth comes new joys, challenges, and responsibilities, not just for children but for you, too.

Within these years, there are two distinct stages: the Early Growth Years (6 to 9) and the Pre-Teen Years (9 to 12). While both phases share the overarching themes of curiosity, independence, and emotional development, they come with unique challenges and opportunities.

As children grow, their developmental milestones shift, and so does your role in their life.

2.2. MIDDLE CHILDHOOD YEARS (6 TO 12 YEARS)

Developmental Comparison - Early Growth & Pre-Teens

Developmental Areas	Early Growth Years 6 to 9 years	Pre-teen Years 9 to 12 years
Physical and Cognitive Expansion	Their energy and coordination increase making it a great time for sports and active play. They start asking "how" and "why" questions about the world.	They experience early signs of puberty both for boys and girls, they improve their problem-solving skills, and a growing ability to think critically.
Social Skills	Friendships become more important, and they learn teamwork and sharing.	Friendships deepen, and peer influence grows stronger. Conflicts, cliques, and social pressures may emerge.
Emotional Growth	They develop emotional regulation but still need help understanding complex feelings.	Mood swings and self-doubt appear, but they're learning to articulate feelings more clearly.
Our Role as a Parent- We Must	Focus on fostering their curiosity and creating a secure environment. We encourage their growing independence by letting them take on small responsibilities, like packing their school bag or helping with chores.	Support their autonomy while staying emotionally available. Give them space to make decisions and learn from their mistakes. Be a sounding board for their ideas and concerns, encouraging open dialogue about friendships, school, and personal challenges.
Remember	We assign small chores like organizing toys or helping with simple tasks.	We guide them in navigating conflicts and understanding the value of healthy friendships.

Figure 14

THE FIRST SECRET: CONNECTION

The growth years are as much about your journey as a parent as they are about children's development. You're transitioning from being their protector to their guide — a role that will evolve but always remain vital.

Together, you'll navigate these years with a mix of structure, freedom, and joy, laying the foundation for the amazing stages to come. We are going to dive deep into 10 topics in detail.

1. How to balance freedom and responsibility?
2. How to focus on academic growth?
3. How to develop emotional intelligence?
4. How to develop social skills and friendships?
5. How to balance screen time in the modern digital age?
6. How to develop physical and mental strength?
7. How to nurture creativity and guide them to build hobbies?
8. How to grow the parent-child bond?
9. How to introduce financial literacy in the middle years?
10. How to prepare the children for adolescence?

2.2.1: Fostering Independence and Responsibility

Middle childhood, spanning the ages of 6 to 12, is a transformative time when our children begin seeking independence while still relying on our guidance. This is the ideal phase to teach them how to balance freedom with responsibility, helping them develop decision-making skills, accountability, and pride in contributing to the family.

Whether the child is just stepping into this stage (6 to 8) or approaching the threshold of adolescence (9 to 12), nurturing

2.2. MIDDLE CHILDHOOD YEARS (6 TO 12 YEARS)

these qualities can set them up for success in the years to come. Let's explore how to guide this process naturally and supportively.

Encouraging Decision-Making and Accountability

As the child starts making choices and forming opinions, our role shifts to being a guide who teaches them how to own their decisions.

1. Start Small: Offer simple, age-appropriate choices, like "Would you like toast or cereal for breakfast?" for younger children, or "Do you want to do your homework before or after your snack?" for older ones.
2. Guide, Don't Dictate: Provide options and let children weigh the outcomes, offering more complex decisions as they grow.
3. Discuss Consequences: Use reflective questions like, "What do you think went well?" or "What might you do differently next time?"
4. Model Decision-Making: Share your thought process for decisions to teach logical reasoning: "I'm deciding between two errands. Let's think about which one is closer to school."

Teaching Accountability can make a difference so,

1. Connect Choices with Outcomes: "When you don't clean up your toys, it's harder to find them later."
2. Praise Accountability: "I'm proud of you for admitting you forgot your homework. That took courage."

As pre-teens (9 to 12) become more independent, encourage them to take responsibility for their decisions. This might mean letting them face natural consequences, such as forgetting to pack their lunch, while supporting them to learn from the experience.

THE FIRST SECRET: CONNECTION

Age-Appropriate Chores and the Value of Contribution

Chores teach children essential life skills, build character, and help them feel like valued members of the family team. It teaches children responsibility and time management. It also instils a sense of belonging and pride in contributing to the family.

Ages 6–8: Feeding pets, sorting laundry, dusting furniture, organizing toys or books, watering plants.

Ages 9–12: Washing dishes, preparing simple snacks, taking out the trash, cleaning their room, assisting with grocery shopping.

We need to encourage them so that it becomes their habit-

a. Set Clear Expectations: "Your job is to put away your shoes when you come home."
b. Make It Fun: Turn chores into games like, "Let's race to see who can tidy up the fastest!"
c. Connect Chores to Contribution: "When you help clean the kitchen, it makes cooking dinner so much easier."
d. Celebrate Efforts: "You did a great job organizing the books — it looks amazing!"

For pre-teens, emphasize the value of their contribution by giving them larger responsibilities, like planning a simple meal or managing their schedule, which fosters independence and pride.

Balancing Freedom and Guidance

Children in this stage need room to experiment, make mistakes, and learn. Striking the right balance between boundaries and autonomy is key to their growth. Offer structured independence and allow them to make decisions within clear boundaries like

"You can ride your bike for 20 minutes but stay on our street." Also encourage problem-solving like "How do you think we can make sure that you don't forget your lunch again?" We need to respect their individuality and celebrate their unique interests, even if they differ from your expectations.

Case Study: Teaching Responsibility Through Chores

Nine-year-old Aria often forgot to pack her lunch, leading to rushed mornings and frustration.

Her parents introduced a "lunch checklist" and encouraged her to pack her lunch the night before.

They praised her efforts when she succeeded: "You remembered your sandwich and snack — great job!"

On days she forgot, they allowed natural consequences: "It's okay to feel hungry — it's a reminder to pack your lunch tomorrow."

Over time, Aria became more organized and prouder of her growing independence.

Quick Activity: Building Accountability

Choose a responsibility: Pick one task children can take on this week, like packing their school bag or setting the dinner table.

Create a Checklist: Work together to create a visual reminder for the task.

Celebrate Success: At the end of the week, praise their effort: "You remembered to pack your bag every day! Great job taking responsibility." This simple activity builds confidence, accountability, and a sense of accomplishment — key ingredients for a successful journey through middle childhood.

The Bigger Picture

Fostering independence and responsibility during middle childhood lays the foundation for self-discipline, resilience, and confidence. For younger children, this involves guiding them gently as they explore their abilities. For pre-teens, it means stepping back to let them take charge while offering guidance when needed.

By teaching children to make decisions, take accountability, and contribute meaningfully, you're equipping them with the tools they'll need to navigate life's challenges with confidence and independence.

2.2.2: Academic Growth: Supporting Learning Without Pressure

Middle childhood marks a critical phase in academic development. During this time, children transition from foundational skills to more structured and complex learning. But success isn't just about grades — it's about nurturing a love for learning, building confidence, and showing them that curiosity is a lifelong superpower.

This chapter is here to help you strike the perfect balance between academic encouragement and setting healthy expectations, creating an environment where learning feels exciting instead of overwhelming.

2.2. MIDDLE CHILDHOOD YEARS (6 TO 12 YEARS)

Balancing Expectations with Encouragement

As homework, tests, and projects enter into the child's world, it's natural to want them to excel. However, too much pressure can lead to stress and diminish their motivation.

Why Balance Matters

- Support Over Judgment: Encouragement fosters intrinsic motivation, while pressure often breeds fear of failure.
- Effort Over Outcome: Praising effort ("You worked so hard!") rather than results ("You're so smart!") helps children persevere and stay resilient.

How to Balance Expectations

1. Set Realistic Goals: Align expectations with their abilities. Focus on progress rather than perfection. "Let's see how much you improve on the next test."
2. Celebrate Effort, Not Just Results: Recognize hard work, even if the outcome isn't perfect: "I'm proud of how much time and thought you put into that project!"
3. Keep Communication Open: Encourage conversations about school. Create a safe space where they can share challenges and successes without fear of judgment.

Also it's possible that kids just don't want to study, so it's very important to create a study schedule at home.

Creating a Supportive Homework Routine

Homework introduces children to time management and organization. A well-structured, supportive routine can make this process smoother and less stressful.

THE FIRST SECRET: CONNECTION

Steps to Build a Homework-Friendly Environment

1. Designate a Workspace: Set up a quiet, distraction-free area with essentials like pencils, paper, and a calendar.
2. Establish Consistent Timing: Create a predictable schedule, such as starting homework after a 30-minute play break. "Let's finish your homework before dinner so we can relax afterward."
3. Break Tasks into Steps: Divide larger assignments into manageable chunks to reduce overwhelm. For a book report, break it into stages: reading, outlining, and writing.
4. Be a Guide, not a Solver: Instead of doing their work, ask guiding questions: "What do you think the next step should be?"

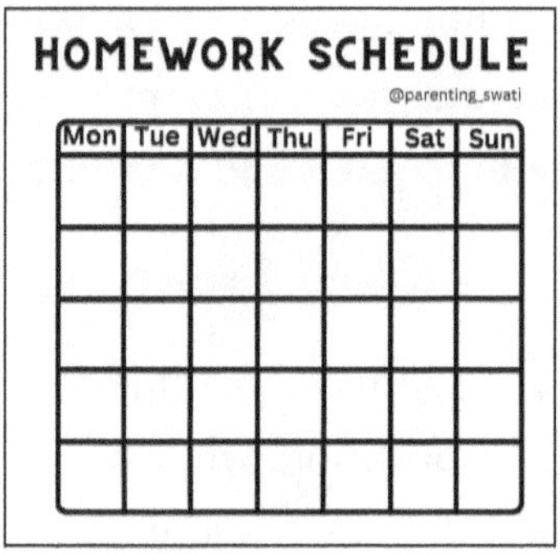

Figure 13

Supporting a Love for Learning

Helping children see learning as fun and meaningful will create a lifelong curiosity about the world.

How to Cultivate a Love for Learning

1. Encourage Exploration Beyond the Classroom: Support their interests with tools like science kits, art supplies, or trips to museums.
2. Connect Learning to Real Life: Show them how schoolwork applies to everyday life. Use cooking to teach fractions or gardening to explore biology.

2.2. MIDDLE CHILDHOOD YEARS (6 TO 12 YEARS)

3. Limit Comparisons: Avoid comparing them to peers or siblings. Celebrate their unique journey and progress.

Pro Tip: Use Binaural Beats for Focus

Listening to 40 Hz binaural beats before studying can enhance concentration and brain activity. Available on YouTube, these beats help in faster and more efficient learning.

Feynman Technique

Simplify what you're learning by teaching it to someone else. Explaining concepts in simple terms deepens understanding and highlights gaps in knowledge.

Case Study: Creating a Stress-Free Learning Environment

Eight-year-old Abhinav struggled with math homework, often becoming frustrated and anxious.

- His parents shifted focus from accuracy to effort: "Let's work on this together and do our best."
- They set up a dedicated study space and added short breaks between tasks to maintain his motivation.
- Over time, Abhinav developed a positive attitude toward math, asking for help when needed and celebrating small wins.

His confidence improved, and his grades climbed — not because of pressure, but because he felt supported and capable.

Quick Activity: The Homework Helper Jar

1. Create a Jar: Fill it with simple, fun tasks children can do during homework breaks. Examples:

THE FIRST SECRET: CONNECTION

- "Do 10 jumping jacks."
- "Draw a doodle of your favorite animal."
- "Tell a joke or a fun fact."

2. Let Them Pick: Encourage children to choose one task during breaks to recharge and refocus.

This small activity adds a playful twist to homework time, making it feel less daunting and more enjoyable.

Figure 14

The Bigger Picture

Middle childhood isn't just about getting good grades — it's about igniting curiosity and building confidence to tackle challenges head-on. By fostering resilience and showing children that learning can be fun, you're shaping their view of education as an exciting journey, not a stressful race.

Through balanced expectations, structured routines, and encouragement, you empower children to take ownership of their learning. Your role isn't just to help them study — it's to inspire them. By valuing effort over results and celebrating curiosity, you're giving them a lifelong gift: the joy of discovery and the confidence to keep growing.

2.2.3: Emotional Intelligence: Helping Children Navigate Feelings

Middle childhood is a time of emotional discovery. As children encounter a broader range of emotions and more complex social interactions, building emotional intelligence (EQ) becomes

2.2. MIDDLE CHILDHOOD YEARS (6 TO 12 YEARS)

essential. EQ — recognizing, understanding, and managing emotions — is the foundation for empathy, resilience, and healthy relationships.

In this lesson, we will learn ways to help children develop emotional skills and navigate social dynamics with confidence and grace.

Teaching Empathy, Resilience, and Self-Awareness

Emotional intelligence goes beyond managing feelings. It's about understanding emotions, how they affect others, and learning to respond thoughtfully. Key components of emotional intelligence are –

1. Empathy: Understanding and sharing others' feelings.
2. Resilience: Bouncing back from setbacks with a positive mindset.
3. Self-Awareness: Recognizing and naming one's emotions.

How to Teach Empathy

1. Model Empathy Daily: Show compassion toward others: "The delivery driver looks tired. Let's thank them for their hard work."
2. Encourage Perspective-Taking: Help children consider others' feelings: "How do you think your friend felt when you didn't share the toy?"
3. Practice Kindness Together: Engage in acts of kindness, like writing thank-you notes, donating toys, or volunteering.

THE FIRST SECRET: CONNECTION

How to Foster Resilience

1. Normalize Failure: Teach children that mistakes are opportunities to learn: "It's okay that you didn't win the game. What did you learn for next time?"
2. Encourage Problem-Solving: Help them brainstorm solutions: "What could you do differently to make up with your friend?"
3. Celebrate Effort Over Results: Focus on perseverance: "I'm proud of how you kept trying, even when it was hard."

How to Build Self-Awareness

1. Teach Emotional Vocabulary: Help children label their emotions: "It seems like you're frustrated because the puzzle isn't fitting. Is that right?"
2. Encourage Reflection: Ask open-ended questions about their feelings: "What made you feel happy today? What made you feel upset?"
3. Use Emotion Charts: Visual aids can help children identify and express emotions effectively.

Handling Peer Influence and Social Dynamics

Friendships take center stage in middle childhood, bringing the joys of connection but also challenges like peer pressure and social conflicts.

Understanding Peer Influence

1. Children seek approval and begin exploring their identity outside the family.
2. Positive vs. Negative Peer Influence: Peers can inspire teamwork and kindness or encourage unkind behavior and risk-taking.

2.2. MIDDLE CHILDHOOD YEARS (6 TO 12 YEARS)

How to Handle Peer Influence

1. Build a Secure Home Foundation: When children feel safe and valued at home, they're less likely to succumb to negative peer pressure: "Remember, you can always talk to me if something feels wrong."
2. Role-Play Scenarios: Practice responses to peer pressure: "What could you say if a friend asks you to do something you're not comfortable with?"
3. Teach Assertiveness: Encourage children to express their feelings respectfully: "I don't like that idea. Let's do something else."

Navigating Social Dynamics

1. Encourage Healthy Friendships: Discuss what makes a good friend: "How does your best friend make you feel? That's how you know it's a healthy friendship."
2. Address Bullying Promptly: Teach children to recognize and report bullying: "If someone is mean to you repeatedly, it's important to tell an adult."
3. Guide Conflict Resolution: Help them resolve disagreements peacefully: "Let's practice how to tell your friend how you feel without being hurtful."

Case Study: Building Emotional Intelligence Through Reflection

Nine-year-old Anika felt left out when her friends didn't invite her to a playdate. She came home in tears, saying, "Nobody likes me!"

- Her mother validated her feelings: "I see you're feeling hurt. It's okay to feel this way."

THE FIRST SECRET: CONNECTION

- Together, they reflected on her emotions and brainstormed possible reasons: "Could it be they had a smaller group this time? What might you say to your friends about how you feel?"
- They created solutions, such as inviting friends over and building confidence with positive affirmations.

Anika felt supported and learned to navigate her feelings while improving communication with her friends.

Quick Activity: Emotional Jar

1. Create an Emotional Jar: Fill a jar with slips of paper, each labeled with an emotion (e.g., happy, sad, angry, excited).
2. Draw and Discuss: Have your child pick a slip and describe a time they felt that emotion. Talk about the cause of the feeling and how they handled it.

Figure 15

3. Reflect Together: "What made you feel that way? Is there something you'd do differently next time?"

This activity builds emotional vocabulary, encourages self-awareness, and fosters open communication.

The Bigger Picture

Emotional intelligence is like a superpower children will use forever. By teaching them empathy, resilience, and self-awareness, you're giving them tools to handle challenges, build strong relationships, and understand themselves better.

Helping children recognize and manage their emotions strengthens their social skills and deepens your bond with them. Your guidance becomes their emotional compass, steering them through life's ups and downs with confidence and grace.

By nurturing emotional intelligence, you're shaping a compassionate, confident, and self-aware individual who will thrive in life's challenges and connections.

2.2.4: Social Skills and Friendships – Building Healthy Relationships and Navigating Challenges

Friendships are the spice of life — and middle childhood is when kids start adding a lot of flavor. From swapping snacks at lunch to negotiating who gets the swing first, these years are packed with lessons on teamwork, empathy, and conflict resolution. Sure, it's messy sometimes (hello, playground drama), but it's all part of growing up.

Let's explore how we can help children build strong friendships and handle the inevitable ups and downs of social life with confidence and kindness.

Friendship 101: Why These Bonds Matter

Friendships in middle childhood are like training wheels for life, teaching kids how to share, resolve conflicts, and navigate emotions — all while having fun. These relationships aren't just about playdates; they're crucial for developing self-esteem and social skills.

THE FIRST SECRET: CONNECTION

The Psychology of Friendships

Erik Erikson's Industry vs. Inferiority Stage

Erikson tells us that kids at this age are all about *competence*. They want to feel successful — not just in school, but also in their social lives.

- The Good News: Friendships build confidence and teach collaboration.
- The Challenge: Social setbacks, like being left out, can lead to feelings of inferiority.

Parents Duty:

- Encourage children to try new group activities, from sports to art clubs.
- Reframe failures as growth opportunities: "It's okay to feel upset about losing a game. What can you do differently next time?"

Strategies for Social Success

You can't control the playground politics, but you *can* give children the tools to navigate them.

1. Encourage Empathy: Teach children to see things from another perspective. "How do you think your classmate felt when no one sat with them? What could you do to help?"
2. Praise Effort, Not Just Outcomes: Celebrate your children's attempts at building relationships, even if they're not perfect. "You were brave to introduce yourself to the new kid. That's a big step!"

3. Teach Conflict Resolution: Help children practice expressing their feelings calmly and respectfully. Role-Play: "If someone interrupts you in a game, you could say, 'I feel upset when I don't get a turn. Can we try again?'"
4. Build Resilience Against Peer Pressure: Reinforce their confidence to say no when needed."It's okay to stand up for what's right, even if your friends disagree. That shows real strength."

The Power of Modelling

Kids are like little sponges — they watch what you do and absorb it.

Albert Bandura's Social Learning Theory: Children learn social behaviors by observing others. If you model kindness, inclusivity, and patience, children are more likely to follow suit. Show how to include others in conversations: "I noticed you haven't met [new neighbor]. Let's invite them to join us for a chat!"

John Bowlby's Attachment Theory: A secure parent-child bond gives kids the confidence to explore relationships outside the family. Be their emotional safe haven: "I'm always here to listen if you need to talk about something."

What About Peer Drama?

Friendship hiccups are inevitable, but they're also teachable moments.

1. Encourage Healthy Friendships: Discuss what makes a good friend: kindness, trust, and shared fun. "How does your

THE FIRST SECRET: CONNECTION

best friend make you feel? That's how you know it's a good friendship."
2. Address Bullying Head-On: Teach children to recognize and report bullying. "If someone is being mean to you repeatedly, it's important to tell an adult. You deserve to feel safe."
3. Guide Conflict Resolution: Help children find solutions without resorting to blame. "Let's practice saying, 'I felt left out when you didn't invite me to play. Can we include everyone next time?'"

Case Study: Riya's Recess Breakthrough

Eight-year-old Riya felt left out during recess, often sitting alone while others played.

- Encouraged her to join a group art project to build her confidence.
- Modeled inclusive behavior at home by involving her in family decisions.
- Reassured her during bedtime chats, helping her process feelings and brainstorm ways to connect with peers.

With a little encouragement and practice, Riya started making new friends and enjoying recess instead of dreading it.

Quick Activity: The Friendship Map

Objective: Help children reflect on and strengthen their friendships.

1. Grab a piece of paper and create a "map" of their social world.
2. Write down the names of friends, classmates, or teammates.
3. Next to each name, ask your child to write or draw:
    - *One thing they like about that friend.*

2.2. MIDDLE CHILDHOOD YEARS (6 TO 12 YEARS)

   o *One way they can show kindness or appreciation to that friend.*
4. Discuss why these friendships matter and brainstorm ways to nurture them.

This activity fosters gratitude and encourages children to value and maintain their connections.

The Bigger Picture

Middle childhood is where kids learn the building blocks of relationships — empathy, communication, and resilience. With your guidance (and a few role-plays), they'll navigate friendships with kindness and confidence.

Remember, it's not about solving every playground squabble for them. It's about giving them the tools to handle challenges on their own while knowing you're always there to support them.

And hey, if they bring you a story about playground drama? Lean in, listen, and resist the urge to jump in with solutions right away. Sometimes, all they need is a sounding board and a hug. ❋

2.2.5: Screen Time and Digital Boundaries – Striking the Right Balance

Let's face it — screens are as much a part of childhood today as crayons and swings were in the past. Whether it's Minecraft marathons, endless YouTube videos, or texting their way through a weekend, kids are hooked. And managing screen time? That's where you come in, armed with love, limits, and maybe a deep breath.

THE FIRST SECRET: CONNECTION

Here's how to create digital boundaries that keep screen time from taking over without turning into the dreaded "No Fun Police."

The Screen Time Tug-of-War

Why are screens so addictive? Blame dopamine — the "feel-good" chemical our brains release when we score points, get likes, or watch funny videos. For kids, this creates a feedback loop, making logging off as tough as finding a missing sock.

Adding to the challenge, kids' self-control and focus — key executive functions — are still developing. This makes screens even harder to resist, leaving parents feeling like they're in an Olympic event just to manage screen time.

Mastering the Art of Digital Boundaries

Think of managing screen time as teaching children how to savor their tech treats without bingeing. The key is creating a balanced relationship with technology that includes safety, structure, and lots of non-digital fun.

1. Set Clear Screen Limits (With a Smile): Here's a trick: use the 4-P Rule to guide screen time decisions:
   - Purpose: Is it for learning, entertainment, or creativity?
   - Program: Is the content age-appropriate and enriching?
   - Parental Presence: Can you co-watch or discuss it later?
   - Proportion: Is it balanced with activities like reading or playing outside?
2. Suggested Limits:
   - Ages 6–8: 1–1.5 hours of recreational screen time daily.

2.2. MIDDLE CHILDHOOD YEARS (6 TO 12 YEARS)

- Ages 9–12: Up to 2 hours, split between fun, learning, and creative tasks.

3. Create Screen-Free Zones: Certain places are sacred — keep screens out of them.
   - Dining Table: Food and family > screens.
   - Bedrooms: A screen-free sleep zone means better rest and fewer "just one more episode" battles.
4. Establish Tech-Free Times: Set specific times when screens are off-limits, like during meals or an hour before bedtime. Bonus: this gives you uninterrupted family time and helps everyone wind down without glowing distractions.
5. Model Healthy Habits: Kids learn from watching you (even when they're pretending not to).
   - Show them intentional tech use: "I'm turning off my phone so we can chat over dinner."
   - Limit your own screen time during family moments.
6. Offer Exciting Offline Alternatives: Screens can't compete with a family board game or an impromptu karaoke session. Create tech-free rituals like weekend hikes or reading marathons to balance the digital pull.
7. **Screen Time Agreement**

Rule	Agreed Time (Daily)	Parent Signature	Child Signature
YouTube/Netflix	1 hour		
Homework on devices	30 minutes		
Social Media	Only on weekends		

Introducing Responsible Technology Use

Handing over a tablet isn't just about entertainment — it's a chance to teach children how to use technology thoughtfully and safely.

Teach Digital Literacy

- Privacy Awareness: "Never share your name, address, or school online."
- Spotting Fake News: "Let's double-check this info. How do we know it's true?"
- Cyberbullying: Encourage children to talk about any uncomfortable online experiences. Reassure them you're always there to help.

Online Safety 101

Keeping children safe online doesn't have to feel like spying — it's about building trust and setting clear expectations.

1. Parental Controls: Use device settings to restrict access to inappropriate content and set usage timers.
2. Know Their Apps: Familiarize yourself with their favorite games and platforms. (Yes, even if Roblox makes no sense to you.)
3. Family Tech Agreement: Create rules together, like:
    - *No screens during meals.*
    - *Get permission before downloading apps.*
    - *Screen time ends 1 hour before bedtime.*

Case Study: Arjun's Tech Tune-Up

Nine-year-old Aditya spent hours gaming, leading to arguments when it was time to unplug.

2.2. MIDDLE CHILDHOOD YEARS (6 TO 12 YEARS)

1. Introduced a tech schedule: 1 hour of gaming after homework.
2. Offered fun offline alternatives, like puzzles and biking.
3. Established a family rule: no screens during meals or after 8 PM.

Aditya learned to manage his screen use, and family life got a whole lot smoother.

The Bigger Picture

Screens aren't the enemy — they're tools. Teaching children how to use them responsibly gives them life skills like self-regulation, prioritization, and online safety.

When managed thoughtfully, technology can spark creativity, learning, and connection. With your guidance, children will master the art of balancing screen time with real-life adventures.

Quick Activity: The Screen Time Calendar

Objective: Help kids balance screen time with other activities.

1. Grab a blank calendar and mark daily screen-free zones (e.g., during meals, before bed).
2. Let them decorate it with stickers or drawings for extra motivation.
3. Review the week together: "What worked? What could we tweak?"

Figure 16

This shared activity encourages accountability and teaches children to balance their own time.

Managing screen time is like teaching children to ride a bike — it takes practice, patience, and the occasional wobble. With thoughtful limits and fun alternatives, you're not just keeping the tech monster at bay; you're showing children how to enjoy the digital world without getting lost in it.

So go ahead, set those boundaries, and enjoy a game of charades instead of endless scrolling. Trust me, children will thank you — eventually. 🌸

2.2.6: Physical and Mental Health – Growing Strong Inside and Out

Middle childhood, spanning ages 6 to 12, is a time of rapid growth — physically, mentally, and emotionally. While children may not always realize it, their daily choices (with a little guidance from you!) shape their lifelong wellness. This stage, covering both the active curiosity of 6 to 9 and the self-awareness of 9 to 12, is perfect for instilling habits that stick. With a mix of fun, conversation, and teamwork, you can create a foundation for health that feels natural and joyful.

Why Physical and Mental Health Go Hand-in-Hand

Active play doesn't just build stronger muscles; it's also a stress-buster that boosts mood and sharpens focus. Similarly, teaching kids to navigate their emotions builds resilience and supports better decision-making. A holistic approach means addressing both body and mind, creating a balance that helps children thrive.

2.2. MIDDLE CHILDHOOD YEARS (6 TO 12 YEARS)

What Psychology Teaches Us About Health

Kids learn by watching you. If you're reaching for the carrot sticks or lacing up for a family walk, children are more likely to follow suit. Younger kids (6 to 9) mimic your habits with enthusiasm, while older ones (9 to 12) start asking "why" and understanding logical connections.

Make Health Fun and Family-Centric

- Create challenges like "Family Step Count Showdown" or "Eat the Rainbow" for 21 days.
- Use a "Healthy Choices Chart" to track simple habits like drinking water, eating veggies, or spending time outside.

Making Active Play a Daily Adventure

Children need movement, but a simple "go play outside" doesn't always work. Tailor activities to their developmental stage:

1. Unstructured Play (6–9): Encourage free exploration like biking, tag, or creative games.
2. Gamify Movement (All Ages): Set up backyard obstacle courses or scavenger hunts. Dance-offs to favorite tunes are fun for everyone!
3. Team Sports (9–12): Soccer, swimming, or dance classes teach coordination, teamwork, and resilience wrapped in fun.

Nourishing Healthy Eating Habits (Without the Drama)

Introducing healthy foods doesn't have to be a battle of wills.

1. Traffic Light System:
    - *Green Light Foods: Eat often (fruits, veggies, whole grains).*

THE FIRST SECRET: CONNECTION

- *Yellow Light Foods: Enjoy sometimes (cheese, granola bars).*
- *Red Light Foods: Treat sparingly (sugary snacks, fried goodies).*

This system is simple, visual, and easy for kids to grasp.

2. Get Them Involved:
   - Let younger kids (6–9) help stir the pancake batter or pick a veggie at the market.
   - Encourage older kids (9–12) to choose recipes and assist with meal prep.
3. Sneak in the Good Stuff:
   - *Blend spinach into a smoothie or add shredded carrots to pasta sauce — it's a win-win!*

Supporting Mental Well-Being

As kids grow, their emotions deepen. Teaching them to recognize and manage feelings is just as important as teaching them to tie their shoes.

How to Encourage Emotional Health

1. Talk About Feelings: Help them label emotions: "It sounds like you're frustrated. Want to tell me more about it?"
2. Introduce Coping Tools: Try deep breathing exercises, drawing, or journaling as ways to calm down or express emotions.
3. Build Resilience: Teach them the power of *yet*: "You can't climb the monkey bars *yet*, but with practice, you'll get there!"

2.2. MIDDLE CHILDHOOD YEARS (6 TO 12 YEARS)

Spotting and Supporting Stress

Sometimes, stress sneaks in quietly. Look for changes like irritability, withdrawal, or trouble sleeping. If you notice these signs:

1. Start the Conversation: "I've noticed you seem upset lately. Let's figure out what's going on together."
2. Normalize Seeking Help: Share stories of how asking for help — from a teacher, counselor, or friend — makes us stronger, not weaker.

PRO TIP: Lunch Box Love Notes

- Write a simple "You're amazing!" or "Good luck on your test!" on a sticky note.
- Add fun riddles or jokes to brighten children's lunchtime.
- Include motivational quotes like, "Dream big, little one!"

Case Study: Priya's Path to Balance

Ten-year-old Priya stopped playing outside and became withdrawn after school.

1. Introduced evening walks as a no-pressure way to connect and unwind.
2. Reintroduced movement with Priya's favorite music, turning dance sessions into a daily ritual.
3. Encouraged journaling for private emotional expression.

Priya gradually became more active, engaged, and communicative, boosting her physical and mental well-being.

THE FIRST SECRET: CONNECTION

Quick Activity

🌈 Eat a Rainbow Every Day! 🌈

Eat a colorful plate of fruits and veggies daily for 21 Days.

Figure 17

Each color provides unique nutrients and health benefits:

- Red 🥕: Boosts heart health (tomatoes, strawberries, red peppers).
- Orange & Yellow 🥕: Great for eyes and immunity (carrots, oranges, mangoes).
- Green 🥦: Packed with vitamins and minerals (spinach, broccoli, cucumbers).
- Blue & Purple 🍇: Supports brain and memory (blueberries, eggplant).
- White 🧄: Fights germs and boosts immunity (onions, garlic, cauliflower).

2.2. MIDDLE CHILDHOOD YEARS (6 TO 12 YEARS)

💡 *Challenge*: Involve your kids! Let them pick a fruit or veggie from each color to build their own rainbow plate. And repeat it for 21 days. Click pictures of your food item and make a scrap file of it.

The Bigger Picture

Teaching children to care for their body and mind, sets them up for a lifetime of wellness. For younger children (6–9), it's about playful introductions to healthy habits. For pre-teens (9–12), it's about deeper understanding and ownership of their choices.

Whether it's a bike ride after school or a family meal full of laughter, these moments create lasting habits. Together, make health a joyful, shared journey that empowers children for years to come.

2.2.7: Nurturing Creativity and Hobbies – Unleashing Children's Unique Spark

Middle childhood, spanning ages 6 to 12, is a time when curiosity blossoms and passions begin to take shape. Whether it's painting wild masterpieces, building LEGO skyscrapers, or writing fantastical stories, this stage is perfect for encouraging creativity and hobbies. These pursuits are not just fun — they're powerful tools for self-expression, critical thinking, and emotional growth.

Let's explore how to nurture creativity and hobbies naturally as children move through the early growth years (6–9) and into the more independent pre-teen stage (9–12).

THE FIRST SECRET: CONNECTION

Why Creativity Matters

Encouraging creativity isn't just about the arts. It's about helping children develop skills that fuel confidence and resilience. When kids create, they learn to:

- Think outside the box.
- Solve problems with imagination.
- Bounce back from mistakes (because not every finger painting is a masterpiece).

For younger children (6–9), creativity might look like experimenting with crayons, inventing games, or building fantastical worlds from blocks. As they grow into pre-teens (9–12), creativity can evolve into more focused pursuits, such as coding, storytelling, or exploring musical instruments.

The Psychology of Creativity

Research confirms what every parent knows intuitively: creativity is essential for a child's development.

- Free Play Enhances Divergent Thinking: Kids who engage in unstructured play become better at brainstorming solutions.
- Structured Activities Refine Skills: Classes or workshops help kids deepen their knowledge in areas they love.
- Balance is Key: A mix of free play and guided learning fosters both imagination and discipline.

Pro Tip: A child who loves tinkering with cardboard forts during free play might thrive in a robotics club — combining creativity with structure.

2.2. MIDDLE CHILDHOOD YEARS (6 TO 12 YEARS)

How to Spark Creativity

1. Spot Their Passions
   Pay attention to what lights them up:
- Are they sketching superheroes?
- Building elaborate forts?
- Writing wild, imaginative stories?

Ask open-ended questions to dive deeper:
- "What's your dream project?"
- "If you could create anything, what would it be?"

2. Balance Free Play with Guided Exploration
- Free Play (6–9): Provide open-ended materials like crayons, building blocks, or cardboard boxes to let their imaginations run wild.
- Guided Exploration (9–12): Enroll them in a pottery class, robotics workshop, or music lessons to refine their skills while encouraging experimentation.

3. Try the 70/30 Rule:
- 70% child-led exploration.
- 30% structured learning.

4. Encourage Experimentation Across Ages
- Younger Kids (6–9): Celebrate effort over outcomes: "Wow, I love how colorful that drawing is!"
- Pre-Teens (9–12): Support perseverance through challenges: "What do you think you can try differently next time?"

Making Creativity a Family Affair

Join In the Fun

THE FIRST SECRET: CONNECTION

Your involvement shows them that creativity is valuable.

- Collaborate on a drawing.
- Build a LEGO city together.
- Turn old cardboard boxes into a spaceship (bonus: it keeps them off screens for an afternoon!).

Encourage Problem-Solving

When they face challenges, don't jump in with the solution. Instead, ask:

- "What do you think could work here?"
- "What would you try next time?"

Case Study: Aarav's Art Adventure

Aarav loved drawing but avoided formal art classes, fearing they'd stifle his creativity.

1. Encouraged him to sketch freely at home with no rules or expectations.
2. Introduced a casual weekend art workshop where he could learn techniques in a playful environment.
3. Focused on celebrating his efforts rather than critiquing the results.

Aarav combined his natural creativity with newfound skills, all while keeping his love for drawing intact.

Practical Tips for Parents

1. Set Up a Creative Corner: Dedicate a small area in your home for arts, crafts, or experiments. Stock it with paints, markers, or recycled materials.

2.2. MIDDLE CHILDHOOD YEARS (6 TO 12 YEARS)

2. Schedule Creativity Time: Set aside 20–30 minutes daily for free play or a hobby — no screens allowed.
3. Encourage "What If" Thinking: Ask playful questions like:
   - *"What if animals could talk? What would they say?"*
   - *"What would a house on the moon look like?"*

Quick Activity: Build a Creative Corner

Objective: Create a space where children can explore their imagination anytime.

1. Gather Supplies: Include paints, crayons, building blocks, or whatever they love.
2. Make It Theirs: Let them decorate the corner with their drawings or a sign that says "(Children's Name)'s Workshop."
3. Celebrate Creations: Display their artwork or projects on a family wall of fame.

The Bigger Picture

Nurturing creativity in middle childhood isn't about producing the next Picasso or Einstein. It's about helping children find joy in exploration, build confidence in their abilities, and discover their unique voice.

Remember: Creativity is messy. Sometimes it's a glitter explosion; other times, it's a half-finished drawing that gets abandoned for a game of tag. The magic lies in the journey, not the outcome.

So, stock up on craft supplies, clear some space on the fridge for their "masterpieces," and join them in their world of wonder. Because those lopsided pancake sculptures? They're not just projects — they're memories. ✺

2.2.8: The Growing Parent-Child Bond – Connecting Through the Chaos

As children grow, so does your relationship with them. Middle childhood is a golden time to nurture this bond — before the whirlwind of teenage years arrives. These years are about building trust, fostering communication, and sharing those simple yet profound moments that leave you both smiling.

Let's explore how to keep that connection strong, even when life gets busy.

Why the Bond Evolves

Your once-little sidekick is growing up, forming their own opinions, building friendships, and learning to navigate the world. For younger children (6–9), you're their go-to for guidance and reassurance. By the pre-teen years (9–12), they may seem more independent, but your role as their safe harbor remains vital. Whether it's a hug after a tough day or a late-night chat, you're still the person they turn to for support.

Keeping Communication Open

For 6 to 8 Years

1. Listen Like You Mean It: Show them their voice matters. Drop distractions (yes, even the phone) and reflect what they're saying:
    - *"It sounds like you were frustrated during recess."*

2. Shake Up the Questions: Instead of the usual "How was school?" try:
    - *"What made you laugh today?"*

2.2. MIDDLE CHILDHOOD YEARS (6 TO 12 YEARS)

- *"If you could switch places with your teacher, what's the first rule you'd change?"*

For 9 to 12 Years

1. Create a Judgment-Free Zone: Pre-teens often wrestle with mistakes and self-doubt. Respond with understanding:
   - *Instead of: "Why didn't you do your homework?"*
   - *Try: "What got in the way of finishing it? Let's figure it out together."*
2. Dive Into Deeper Topics: Ask open-ended questions about their growing interests and challenges:
   - *"What's one thing you'd change about school if you could?"*

Finding Bonding Moments in Busy Days

1. Routine Rituals: Turn everyday moments into opportunities to connect.
   - Dinner Chats: Share one "high" and one "low" from the day.
   - Bedtime Reflections: Snuggle up and talk about their dreams or read a chapter of a shared book.
2. One-on-One Time: Even 10 minutes can make a difference.
   - *Go for a bike ride.*
   - *Bake cookies together.*
   - *Play a quick card game.*
3. Special Solo Dates: Carve out gadget-free, judgment-free time with just one child. A walk in the park or grabbing an ice cream cone can work wonders. Pro Tip: Leave correction at home. This is about connection, laughter, and memories.

THE FIRST SECRET: CONNECTION

- *The Magic of Play and Humor:* Dive into their world — whether it's building a LEGO fortress or kicking a soccer ball. Play helps bridge the gap between their world and yours. Shared laughter is the ultimate icebreaker. Start a family tradition like silly storytime, funny face contests, or "family joke night." The goofier, the better.

Psychological Backing for Bonding

Your consistent emotional presence builds trust and security. Kids make "bids" for connection every day — like asking you to look at their drawing or seeking your help with a game.

- *Show genuine interest:* "Wow, that's a cool drawing! Tell me about it."
- *Offer encouragement:* "You're doing great — keep going!"

The Power of Words: Shaping Minds and Emotions

The famous scientist, Dr. Masaru Emoto, suggests that water crystals respond to emotions and words. Positive stimuli, like kind words or prayers, formed beautiful crystals, while negative words created chaotic ones. Given that the human body is 75% water, like water, children absorb and retain the tone and energy of what is said to them. Positive affirmations nurture confidence, resilience, and emotional well-being. Emoto's work reminds us: Words don't just shape water crystals — they shape lives. Speak with care; your words hold transformative power.

Innovative Bonding Idea: The Connection Jar

Here's a simple, fun way to create shared moments.

What You'll Need:

2.2. MIDDLE CHILDHOOD YEARS (6 TO 12 YEARS)

- A jar
- Slips of paper
- A marker

What to Do:
1. Write simple bonding activities on each slip:
   - *"Build a fort together."*
   - *"Go on a nature walk."*
   - *"Share your funniest memory."*
2. Let them pick one whenever you have time together.

Bonus: It's a fun surprise for both of you!

<u>Case Study: Maya and Vedant's Breakfast Bond</u>

Maya, a busy working parent, felt disconnected from her nine-year-old, Vedant.

1. Started a Saturday morning "unplugged" breakfast where they shared their week.
2. Began reading the same book as Vedant, chatting about it before bed.
3. Dedicated 10 minutes every evening for a quick check-in.

Vedant began sharing his thoughts and feelings more openly, strengthening their relationship despite the hectic schedule.

Quick Activity: The Conversation Starter Deck

Objective: Make family conversations easy and fun.

What You'll Need:

- Index cards or slips of paper.

THE FIRST SECRET: CONNECTION

1. Write a question or topic on each card. Examples:
   - *"What's the funniest thing that happened to you this week?"*
   - *"If you could visit any planet, which one would it be and why?"*
   - *"What's one thing you're proud of?"*
2. Pull a card during meals, car rides, or downtime.

   It's a simple way to spark meaningful conversations without forcing it.

The Bigger Picture

Middle childhood is about planting seeds of trust, connection, and love. These years are a time to lay the foundation for the open communication and mutual respect that will carry you through the teenage years and beyond.

- Be Present: Even a few focused moments can make a big impact.
- Create Rituals: Small, consistent traditions matter.
- Celebrate Their Growth: Let them know you see and appreciate who they're becoming.

In the hustle of daily life, these little moments of connection are priceless. They're the memories children will hold onto — and so will you. ✶

2.2.9: Introducing Financial Literacy – Building Smart Money Habits

Middle childhood, spanning ages 6 to 12, is the perfect time to introduce the foundational concepts of financial literacy. During this stage, children begin to understand the value of effort, saving, and spending. By teaching them about money in a practical and relatable way, you're equipping them with skills that will serve them for life.

Whether child is just beginning to grasp basic concepts (6–8) or is ready to manage small budgets and plan for goals (9–12), this chapter will guide you on how to nurture financial awareness in an age-appropriate and culturally relevant way.

Building Financial Awareness and Responsibility

Children are naturally curious about money — what it is, how it's earned, and how it's spent. Use this curiosity to build their understanding and confidence.

1. Make It Tangible (Ages 6–8): Use coins and currency notes like ₹10, ₹20, or ₹50 to explain the basics of money.
   - *Example: "If you save ₹5 every day for a week, you'll have ₹35 by the end of the week."*
2. Introduce Earning and Saving (Ages 9–12): Encourage them to save for specific goals, like a cricket bat or a book they want, using their allowance or pocket money.
   - *Example: "If you save ₹100 from your pocket money each week, you'll have ₹400 by the end of the month to buy your favorite board game."*
3. Explain Needs vs. Wants: Help them understand the difference between essentials and luxuries.
   - *"Buying rice and dal for the house is a need, but chocolates and chips are wants. Both are okay, but we need to plan for the extras."*

THE FIRST SECRET: CONNECTION

Teaching Financial Responsibility:

- Connect Effort with Rewards

1. For Younger Kids (6–8): Give small rewards for completed tasks, like saving part of their pocket money to buy a small treat. "If you save ₹20 this week, you can buy a packet of your favorite biscuits."
2. For Older Kids (9–12): Offer more responsibility, such as managing their allowance for specific expenses like snacks, stationery, or gifts.
   - Encourage Goal Setting- Create a simple savings chart with visual goals. Like "You're saving ₹500 for a new book. Let's mark every ₹50 you save on this chart!"
   - Model Smart Money Habits- Share your financial decisions: "We're comparing prices at two stores to save money," or "We're saving this month for a family trip."

Age-Appropriate Money Skills

Ages 6–8:
- Counting and Saving: Use a piggy bank or jars labelled "Spend," "Save," and "Give-Charity."
- Basic Transactions: Let them hand over money at the store for small items like ₹10 snacks to understand purchases.

Ages 9–12:
- Budgeting: Teach them to manage their allowance, dividing it between savings and spending.
- Tracking Expenses: Help them record where their money goes, using a notebook or a simple app.

2.2. MIDDLE CHILDHOOD YEARS (6 TO 12 YEARS)

- Earning Opportunities: Encourage small entrepreneurial projects, like making greeting cards to sell or assisting neighbors with chores for a small fee.

How to Encourage Financial Participation?

1. Set Clear Expectations: Teach them the importance of consistency.
    - *"If you save ₹50 every week, you'll have ₹200 by the end of the month."*
2. Make Saving Fun: Create challenges to inspire saving.
    - *"Let's see who can save ₹100 first — me or you!"*
3. Connect Money to Real-Life Experiences: Take them shopping to teach budgeting and price comparison.
    - *"If we have ₹500 for fruits, which ones should we buy to stay within the budget?"*
4. Celebrate Successes: Acknowledge their effort with praise.
    - *"You saved ₹300 and bought your storybook — great job planning for it!"*

Case Study: Aarav's Savings Journey

Aarav, an 8-year-old, wanted a cricket bat that cost ₹800.
- Step 1: His parents encouraged him to save ₹100 each week from his pocket money.
- Step 2: They matched his savings by contributing ₹100 for every ₹200 he saved to motivate him.
- Step 3: Aarav kept a chart to track his progress and felt excited as he got closer to his goal.

When Aarav finally bought the cricket bat, he understood the value of saving and the satisfaction of working towards a goal.

THE FIRST SECRET: CONNECTION

Quick Activity: The Savings Jars

Objective: Teach children about saving, spending, and sharing.

1. Materials: Three jars labeled "Spend," "Save," and "Give Charity"
2. How It Works:
   - *Divide their pocket money — for example, ₹100:*
     - ₹50 to "Save" (for a long-term goal).
     - ₹40 to "Spend" (for small treats).
     - ₹10 to "Give" (to help someone or donate to charity).

The Bigger Picture

Teaching financial literacy during middle childhood sets the stage for lifelong money management skills.

- For Younger Kids (6–8): Focus on simple concepts like saving, spending, and earning.
- For Older Kids (9–12): Introduce budgeting, goal setting, and responsible decision-making.

By incorporating financial literacy into daily life, you're not just teaching them about rupees — you're helping them understand the value of effort, patience, and planning. These lessons will grow with them, shaping confident, responsible individuals who can make smart financial choices throughout their lives. And this journey continues in their teenage years and the future to come.

Children who learn to manage money early gain critical life skills that set them up for success.

1. They develop financial responsibility, learning to budget, save, and spend wisely.

2. They build decision-making skills, patience, and the ability to prioritize needs over wants.
3. It helps foster confidence and independence, empowering kids to set and achieve goals.
4. It also enhances critical thinking and problem-solving, preparing them for real-world challenges.
5. These skills contribute to better academic and career outcomes and a balanced relationship with money.
6. It teaches them to have an entrepreneurial mindset.
7. By managing money early, children grow into financially savvy, resilient, and responsible adults.

2.2.10: Celebrating the Growth Years and Preparing for Adolescence

Middle childhood, often called the "growth years," is a time of incredible transformation for both children and parents. This phase bridges the innocence of early childhood and the complexity of adolescence, filled with opportunities to foster independence, nurture creativity, and deepen your parent-child bond.

As this chapter in children's life closes, let's celebrate the milestones, reflect on the journey, and prepare for the exciting years ahead.

Recognizing Growth Beyond Achievements

Middle childhood isn't just about report cards and trophies — it's about the subtle triumphs that shape character:

- For Ages 6–9: Resolving their first argument with a friend or tying their shoes for the first time.

- For Ages 9–12: Baking their first batch of cookies, gaining the courage to speak up in class, or trying something new despite fear.

Celebrate their unique journey by focusing on progress over comparison:

- "You've worked so hard on that project — it's amazing to see how your creativity has grown!"

Your Evolving Role as a Parent

As your child grows, your role shifts from being their nurturer to their coach.

From Nurturer to Coach

- Ages 6–9: Be hands-on but encourage small steps toward independence.
  - *"What do you think we should do next? Let's figure it out together."*
- Ages 9–12: Step back and guide from the sidelines, allowing them to take the lead.
  - *"What's your plan for solving this? I'm here if you need support."*

Fostering Confidence and Resilience

- Allow Risks and Mistakes: Let them stumble and learn from experience.
  - *"It's okay that you didn't get it right this time. What did you learn from trying?"*

- Celebrate Effort Over Results: Reinforce the value of hard work rather than perfection.

Preparing for Adolescence

As the teenage years approach, the dynamics of your relationship will shift again. Middle childhood is the time to lay a strong foundation for trust, open communication, and independence.

Starting the Conversation About Changes: Normalize the physical and emotional changes of adolescence. "Your body and emotions will go through some exciting changes soon. If you ever have questions, I'm always here to chat."

Encouraging Critical Thinking: Begin fostering decision-making skills now. Instead of solving every problem, ask: "What do you think is the best solution? Why?"

Building Trust Gradually: Small Responsibilities: Let them plan part of a family outing or manage their allowance. Collaborative Rules: Work together on boundaries, like screen time limits, so they feel respected.

The Parent-Child Bond: A Foundation for the Future

These years are also about strengthening the bond you'll rely on during the turbulence of adolescence.

Making Time for Connection

- Routine Rituals: Family dinners, bedtime chats, or Sunday morning pancake sessions.

THE FIRST SECRET: CONNECTION

- One-on-One Time: Even 15 minutes of undivided attention can work wonders. Go for a walk, bake cookies, or simply chat about their day.

The Role of Play and Humor

- Play Together: Whether it's a board game or building LEGO towers, these moments foster connection.
- Laugh Often: Share inside jokes, have impromptu dance-offs, or tell silly stories — it's the glue of a strong bond.

Activity: The Trust and Independence Jar

Purpose: Teach responsibility and celebrate small wins.

What You'll Need

- A jar
- Small slips of paper

How It Works

1. Write tasks children can handle independently, like "Pack my lunch" or "Plan a family movie night."
2. Each week, let them pick one slip and take charge of that task.
3. At the end of the week, discuss how it went and celebrate their effort.

Middle childhood is a precious, fleeting phase. It's a time of growth, discovery, and strengthening the parent-child bond.

2.2. MIDDLE CHILDHOOD YEARS (6 TO 12 YEARS)

What You've Taught Them

- Confidence: Through your encouragement, they've learned to take on challenges with bravery.
- Independence: By letting them try, fail, and try again, you've shown them the value of resilience.
- Love: Every laugh, hug, and word of support has built a foundation of unconditional love.

What They've Taught You

- To See the World Anew: Their curiosity and wonder remind you to slow down and savor life.
- To Laugh at the Chaos: Those spilled cereals and mismatched socks are part of the joy.

As you step into the next phase of parenthood, remember:

- Trust the Process: The seeds you've planted during middle childhood will continue to grow.
- Celebrate the Journey: Look back on how far you and your child have come together.

These years aren't just about raising a child; they're about growing together as a family. The road ahead will bring new challenges and triumphs, but you've built the foundation to face them with love, patience, and confidence.

Here's to the incredible adventure of parenting — and to the amazing person your child is becoming. ✨

Section 1
What is Parenting

Section 2
The First Secret Connection

2.1
Foundation Years
1 - 5 Years

2.2
Middle Childhood
6 - 12 Years

2.3
Teenage Years
13 - 18 Years

YOU ARE HERE

Section 3
The Second Secret Care

Section 4
The Third Secret Celebrate

Section 5
Parent Survival Kit
50+ Activities

Your Parenting Journey

2.3 The Teenage Years: A Time of Transformation for Both Parent and Child

Parenting a teenager is a mix of nostalgia for their childhood and excitement (or nervous anticipation) for their future. Your once-small child is now a whirlwind of curiosity, rebellion, vulnerability, and independence. It's natural to feel overwhelmed at times, but remember: these years are also ripe with opportunities to deepen your bond, model resilience, and guide your teen as they grow into a confident, compassionate adult.

Take a deep breath, embrace the imperfection, and let's embark on this transformative journey together.

Understanding Adolescence: The Why Behind the Turmoil

The teenage years are marked by profound changes — physical, emotional, and social. Understanding these shifts can help you approach this stage with empathy and patience.

1. Identity Formation
   Teens are exploring who they are, which often means questioning family values, testing boundaries, and experimenting with different identities.
   Fact: Offer a judgment-free space for exploration. If they want to dye their hair neon green, focus on understanding their motivation: "What inspired you to choose this colour?"

THE FIRST SECRET: CONNECTION

2. Brain Remodelling

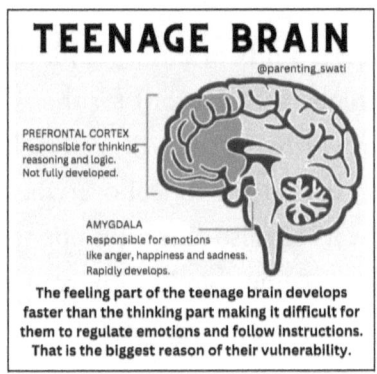

Figure 18

The teenage brain is "under construction," making emotional responses heightened and impulsivity common.

Parenting Tip: Avoid overreacting to impulsive behaviour. Instead, guide them through reflective questioning - "How do you think that decision might impact things next time?"

3. The Peer Factor

- Teens increasingly value their peers' opinions, which can sometimes create friction at home.
- The kids want to look beautiful and loved and this is the time body shaming also starts.
- Parenting Tip: Instead of competing with their social circle, remain a trusted, nonjudgmental ally they can turn to. Communication is the key, talk to them and make them feel loved.

2.3 THE TEENAGE YEARS (13 TO 18 YEARS)

Shifting from Control to Guidance

As your child grows, your role shifts from manager to mentor. This evolution is about fostering independence while maintaining their safety net.

- From Manager to Mentor: Replace directives and be the GPS for children with collaborative discussions. Instead of "You have to finish your homework now," try, "What's your plan for finishing your assignments tonight?" Fact- It's also a great idea to have one safe mentor for the child who the child looks up to and whom you trust as well. Kids will be able to share their feelings and emotions with them openly.
- Be a Safe Harbor: Let them know they can approach you without fear of judgment. "I'm here to help you figure this out, no matter what."
- Show Respect and Trust: Trust their ability to make choices, even if they stumble. This teaches accountability and confidence. "I trust you to decide how to manage your schedule. Let me know if you need any help." Talk to them like little adults and give them reasons and examples when you talk to them.

Teens thrive when they feel competent, autonomous, and connected. Involve them in meaningful decisions and praise their efforts rather than just outcomes. Model calmness during their emotional storms. "I can see you're frustrated. Let's take a few deep breaths together before we talk."

THE FIRST SECRET: CONNECTION

Parenting Teens: A Beautiful Balancing Act

Parenting during the teenage years is all about balance — guiding while letting go, offering structure while embracing freedom, and holding on while trusting them to soar.

Trust the Process: You're planting seeds of resilience, independence, and empathy that will flourish in time. Shared activities like cooking, hiking, or simply watching a favorite movie together can strengthen your bond without pressure.

Stay Curious and Connected: Engaging with your teen's world strengthens your bond and shows you care. Ask about their interests, even if they're unfamiliar to you. "What do you like most about this show? Want to watch an episode together?"

Celebrate Efforts: Perfection isn't the goal — showing up with love, patience, and understanding is what truly matters. Recognize their growth, no matter how incremental. "I'm so proud of how you spoke up during that group project — it shows real leadership."

This stage is a transformative journey for both you and your teen. By building trust, respect, and love, you're shaping a lifelong connection that will only grow stronger.

Embrace the challenges, savour the moments, and celebrate the growth — because these years, though fleeting, create a foundation for an enduring relationship. The best is yet to come.

In this section about transformation and understanding teens better, I am going to unfold -

1. How does the adolescent brain really work?
2. Why does independence become so important to them?

3. How to build emotional intelligence?
4. How to develop parent-teen relationships?
5. How to guide teens in academics and their careers?
6. How do social dynamics and peers influence teenagers?
7. How do screen time and social media impact the teen?
8. How to teach teens about sexuality, relationships and safety?
9. How to help teens enhance their creativity and passion?
10. How to prepare teens for adulthood?

2.3.1: The Adolescent Brain: Navigating Change

Adolescence is like a wild renovation show — your teen's brain is under construction, complete with scaffolding, sparks of creativity, and the occasional emotional wrecking ball. While it might feel chaotic, understanding the science behind these changes can help you approach this stage with empathy, patience, and even a bit of humor. When children are around 12 or 13, an entire new brain is getting created.

What's Happening in the Teenage Brain?

Think of the adolescent brain as a work in progress, fine-tuning itself to prepare for adulthood. Here's what's going on:

1. Remodelling Central: The brain is "pruning" unused pathways and strengthening frequently used ones. Your teen's interests and behaviours are shaping their brain, so those TikTok dances they're obsessed with? They're forming neural pathways, for better or worse.
2. The Slow Prefrontal Cortex: This part of the brain — responsible for planning, self-control, and decision-making

— is still under construction. Expect impulsive decisions, like eating the entire pizza instead of saving you a slice.
3. **The Emotional Limbic System:** The limbic system, which processes emotions, is fully operational and often in overdrive. Mood swings are inevitable. One moment they're laughing hysterically; the next, they're slamming doors.
4. **Dopamine Galore:** Teens experience a dopamine surge, making exciting or risky activities irresistible. They'll prioritize social adventures or adrenaline-pumping experiences over your suggestion to "just relax."

How You Can Support Their Brain's Growth?

Your role is like that of a project manager — guiding, troubleshooting, and occasionally standing back to let them figure things out.

1. **Teach Thoughtful Decision-Making:** Instead of jumping in with solutions, ask questions to help them weigh their options: "What do you think will happen if you skip studying for the test?" Narrate your decision-making process to show how to think things through:
"I'm deciding whether to bake cookies or buy them. Baking sounds fun, but buying might save time. What do you think?"
2. **Help Manage Big Emotions:** Let them know their emotions are real and valid. "It's okay to feel angry about what happened with your friend. Let's talk about how to handle it."
    - **Teach Coping Skills:** Introduce tools like deep breathing, journaling, or physical activity.

2.3 THE TEENAGE YEARS (13 TO 18 YEARS)

- Co-Regulate: Stay calm when they're overwhelmed, offering your presence as an anchor. "I'm here for you. Let's take a moment to breathe together."

3. Encourage Safe Risk-Taking: Channel their need for excitement into productive activities like sports, music, or volunteering. "Let's try hiking that new trail this weekend — it looks challenging!"
4. Balance Freedom with Structure: Offer Flexibility: Teens need room to grow but within clear boundaries. "You can hang out with your friends, but let's set a curfew for 9 PM."

Parenting Insights from Science

Researchers say the brain has an "upstairs" (reasoning) and a "downstairs" (emotions). Teens often operate downstairs because the connection between the two is still forming. Help them climb "upstairs" by guiding them to think through their emotional responses.

The Social Brain Hypothesis: Adolescents prioritize peer relationships as they navigate social dynamics. Support their friendships while encouraging reflection on what makes a healthy connection.

Practical Strategies to Thrive During Brain Chaos

1. Be Their Guide, Not Their Dictator: Collaborate on rules: "How do you want to balance screen time and homework? Let's come up with a plan together."
2. Normalize Mistakes: Frame failure as a growth opportunity: "That didn't work out as planned — what could we try differently next time?"

THE FIRST SECRET: CONNECTION

3. Foster Curiosity: Encourage exploration and critical thinking: "That's an interesting idea. What made you think of it?"

Quick Activity: "Mapping the Brain"

Purpose: Help your teen understand their own brain, making their emotions and decisions feel normal.

What You'll Need

- A large sheet of paper and markers.
- A simple brain diagram (Refer to the Image)

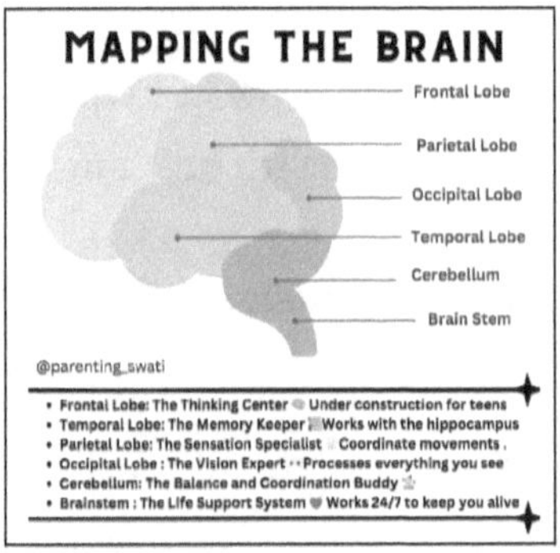

Steps

1. Label the Brain: Include areas like the prefrontal cortex (decision-making) and limbic system (emotions).
2. Annotate: Add simple notes like "Limbic system = strong emotions" or "Prefrontal cortex = planning."
3. Reflect Together: Discuss:
   ◦ "What do you notice about how your brain works?"
   ◦ "How could understanding this help when you feel overwhelmed?"

Figure 19

This activity makes brain science relatable and gives your teen tools to navigate their own emotions and choices.

2.3 THE TEENAGE YEARS (13 TO 18 YEARS)

The Teenage Brain: A Marvel in Motion

The teenage brain is like a construction site — busy, unpredictable, and full of potential. While it may come with impulsivity, mood swings, and the occasional "What were they thinking?" moment, it's also brimming with creativity, curiosity, and growth.

Your patience, empathy, and steady guidance act as the scaffolding for this incredible transformation, helping your teen shape into the adult they're becoming.

Remember, you're not just dealing with a teenager — you're nurturing a future adult who will one day reflect on these years with gratitude for your unwavering support. Here's to navigating the teenage brain — one fascinating, ever-changing connection at a time!

2.3.2: Fostering Independence and Responsibility

The teenage years are a masterclass in balancing acts — for your teen and for you. As they test the waters of independence, your job is to provide them with enough freedom to explore while maintaining the structure they need to thrive. Think of yourself as a lighthouse: a guiding light that helps them navigate through choppy seas without steering the ship for them.

Teens crave autonomy because it helps them:

- Develop Life Skills: They're learning how to manage responsibilities that will carry them into adulthood.
- Build Self-Esteem: Every successful step toward independence reinforces their belief in their capabilities.

At the same time, boundaries are your safety net, ensuring their exploration happens within healthy limits.

How to Encourage Independence While Setting Boundaries

1. Collaborate on Rules
   Teenagers thrive when they feel heard. By involving them in setting boundaries, you show respect for their opinions while still maintaining your role as a guide. Instead of imposing a curfew, ask, "What's a fair curfew for weekends? Let's figure this out together."
2. Gradual Freedoms
   Independence isn't an all-or-nothing deal. Offer more freedom as they demonstrate responsibility. "Since you've been keeping up with your schoolwork, let's extend your curfew by an hour on Saturdays."
3. Model Healthy Boundaries
   Teens learn by watching you. Show them how you manage your own independence and responsibilities. "I'm taking a break now, but I'll finish my work after dinner. Balance is important for everyone."

Helping Teens Manage Time and Personal Goals

The teenage years come with a packed schedule: school, extracurriculars, social life, and (hopefully) some downtime. Helping them master time management is a gift that keeps on giving.

2.3 THE TEENAGE YEARS (13 TO 18 YEARS)

Why Time Management Matters

- Builds Executive Functioning: Planning, prioritizing, and organizing are essential skills for adulthood.
- Reduces Stress: Structure helps teens feel in control of their busy lives.

Figure 20

Practical Strategies

1. Teach Prioritization: Help your teen focus on what needs to be done first. "What's due tomorrow? Let's tackle that before moving on."
2. Use Tools They Like: Introduce planners or apps that match their style. "How about using Google Calendar to keep track of assignments and soccer practice?"
3. Break Big Goals into Small Steps: Guide them in dividing tasks into manageable chunks. For a big project, suggest milestones like "Research this week, draft next week, and final edits the following week."

THE FIRST SECRET: CONNECTION

PRO TIP: Pomodoro Technique for Focus

- Set a timer for 25 minutes of focused work or study.
- Take a 5-minute break to stretch, grab water, or breathe deeply.
- Repeat 4 cycles, then enjoy a longer 15–30 minute break.
- Pro Tip: Use this for kids' homework or your work to stay productive and balanced!

Key Theories to Guide Your Approach

Teens are exploring their identity, and autonomy is a key part of that process. When you let them test independence within boundaries, you're helping them form a solid sense of self.

Your role is to provide just enough support for your teen to succeed — whether it's teaching them to cook or guiding them through a difficult social situation — and then step back as they gain confidence.

Case Study: Balancing Freedom and Responsibility

Fifteen-year-old Maya wanted more freedom to hang out with her friends but struggled to finish her homework on time.

1. Set Expectations: Maya's parents agreed she could go out on weekends, but only if her schoolwork was done first.
2. Provide Tools: Together, they created a homework schedule, breaking tasks into smaller goals.
3. Build Trust: As Maya met her responsibilities, her parents allowed her more freedom.

Maya developed better time-management skills and earned more independence, while her parents gained confidence in her decision-making.

2.3 THE TEENAGE YEARS (13 TO 18 YEARS)

Activity: Responsibility Roadmap

Purpose: Help your teen identify areas where they want more independence and outline how they can earn it.

What You'll Need

- A large sheet of paper or notebook.
- Markers or pens.

Steps

1. Divide the Page: Create two columns: "Responsibilities" and "Freedoms."
2. Brainstorm Together:
   - *Write down current tasks they handle.*
   - *Add freedoms they'd like to gain.*
   - *Example:*
     - Responsibility: "Complete homework without reminders."
     - Freedom: "More screen time on weekends."
3. Set Goals: Agree on specific milestones for earning freedom.
4. Follow-Up: Revisit the roadmap weekly to track progress and adjust as needed.

Growing Independence Together

Fostering independence isn't just about giving your teen more freedom — it's about teaching them how to handle it with care and responsibility. Through trust, guidance, and accountability, you're shaping them into self-reliant, confident individuals ready to take on life's challenges.

This journey isn't just theirs; it's yours too. You're learning to let go, celebrate their milestones, and tackle challenges side by side.

Every small victory is a step forward for both of you. Embrace the process, savor the growth, and cherish the moments — together, you're building a foundation for their future and a bond that lasts a lifetime.

2.3.3: Building Emotional Intelligence

Ah, the teenage years — a time of intense emotions, passionate outbursts, and occasional eye rolls that could power a wind turbine. But beneath the mood swings and drama lies an incredible opportunity to help your teen grow into an emotionally intelligent adult. By fostering empathy, resilience, and self-awareness, you're not just managing meltdowns; you're shaping a future filled with confident, compassionate decision-makers.

Emotional intelligence (EQ) is like a social superpower. Teens with high EQ can navigate conflicts, manage stress, and form meaningful relationships. It's not about eliminating emotions but learning to understand and channel them constructively.

The Building Blocks of Emotional Intelligence

1. Empathy: Empathy is the ability to step into someone else's shoes — without asking, "Ew, where have these been?"
   - Model It: Show understanding in your interactions. "I can see you're frustrated about your group project. How can you talk to your classmates about this?"

- Encourage Perspective-Taking: Prompt your teen to think about others' feelings. "How do you think your friend felt when you canceled your plans at the last minute?"
2. Resilience: Resilience is bouncing back after life hands you lemons — or just a really bad grade.
    - Normalize Failure: Help them see mistakes as stepping stones. "Not making the team is tough, but it's just one moment. Let's work on improving for next time."
    - Encourage Problem-Solving: Guide, don't solve. "What's one thing you can do differently for the next test?"
3. Self-Awareness: Self-awareness is knowing what you're feeling — and not just shouting, "I'M FINE!"
    - Journaling: Encourage them to write down their thoughts and emotions.
    - Labeling Emotions: Help them articulate what they're feeling.
        - *Example: "You seem anxious about tomorrow's game. Is that how you're feeling?"*

Navigating Mood Swings and Stress

Adolescence is basically a rollercoaster — except you didn't buy the tickets, and the ride doesn't come with seatbelts.

Understanding Mood Swings

- The Science: The prefrontal cortex (rational thinking) is still a work in progress, while the limbic system (emotions) is in overdrive.
- The Result: Teens might cry over spilled milk — or slam a door because "nobody understands."

THE FIRST SECRET: CONNECTION

Strategies to Cope

1. Create a Safe Space- "It's okay to feel angry. Let's talk when you're ready."
2. Teach Emotional Regulation -Introduce mindfulness techniques, like deep breathing or visualization. "Let's take five deep breaths together before we figure this out."
3. Recognize Stress Triggers- Break big tasks into manageable chunks. Instead of "Study for your exams," try "Let's tackle math today and history tomorrow."

Encouraging Healthy Outlets

Give emotions a positive outlet to keep them from boiling over.

- Creative Hobbies: Painting, journaling, or playing an instrument.
- Physical Activity: Yoga, biking, or team sports.
- Relaxation Techniques: Deep breathing, meditation apps, or even taking a walk.

Helpful Concepts and Tools

1. EFT (Emotional Freedom Technique) for Stress Relief
   - For Kids: Teach them to gently tap on their collarbone or the side of their hand while repeating affirmations like, "I feel calm and safe."
   - For Parents: Tap on pressure points (side of hand, under eyes, etc.) while repeating positive statements like, "I can handle this with ease."
2. The Mood Meter
   Help your teen pinpoint their emotions using a color-coded chart:

2.3 THE TEENAGE YEARS (13 TO 18 YEARS)

- Red: High energy, low pleasantness (anger, frustration).
- Blue: Low energy, low pleasantness (sadness, disappointment).
- Green: Low energy, high pleasantness (calm, contentment).
- Yellow: High energy, high pleasantness (excitement, joy).
- Pro Tip: Apps- "*How We Feel*" make this fun and interactive.

Case Study: Helping a Teen Handle Stress

Riya, 15, was overwhelmed by exam stress and started snapping at everyone at home.

1. Validated Feelings: "I know exams feel stressful. Let's figure this out together."
2. Introduced Mindfulness: Guided her in 5-minute deep-breathing exercises daily.
3. Created a Plan: Helped break her study schedule into smaller, manageable tasks.

Riya felt more in control, performed better on her exams, and began asking for help when overwhelmed.

Weekly Mood Tracker (Graph Style)

Purpose: Track your moods over the week and spot patterns.

How to Do It

1. Draw Your Graph:
   - *X-axis: Days of the week (Mon to Sun).*
   - *Y-axis: Mood levels (1 = Very Low to 5 = Very High).*
2. Track Daily Mood:

THE FIRST SECRET: CONNECTION

- ○ *At the end of each day, mark a dot on the graph based on your mood.*
- ○ *Connect the dots to see how your mood changes over the week.*

Figure 21

3. Reflect:
   - ○ *"What made me feel good?"*
   - ○ *"What lowered my mood?"*
   - ○ *"What can I do next week to feel better?"*

Why It Helps: A quick visual to understand mood patterns and make positive changes. 🎇

🖊 Pro Tip: Add colors or symbols for each mood to make it creative and fun! 🎨

A Lifelong Toolbox

Helping your teen develop emotional intelligence is like handing them a life toolkit. They'll still encounter challenges, but with empathy, resilience, and self-awareness, they'll know how to face them with grace and strength.

Parenting teens isn't about perfection — it's about progress. Be there, be patient, and when you get an eye roll, just remember — it's their way of saying, "Thanks, Mom/Dad — you're doing great."

By nurturing emotional intelligence, you're giving your teen a lifelong gift: a compass for understanding themselves and building meaningful relationships. It's a legacy of emotional strength they'll carry forever.

2.3.4: The Parent-Teen Relationship

Ah, the teenage years — a time when your once chatty, cuddly child might transform into a headphone-wearing enigma who communicates in grunts and eye rolls. But don't worry — beneath that occasional exasperation is a teen who still deeply values your support (even if they won't admit it). This chapter is all about keeping the connection alive, navigating conflicts, and building a relationship that can withstand slammed doors and hormonal hurricanes.

Even if your teen brings up topics like "vaping" or "alcohol", don't jump the gun. Take a breath. This is your chance to connect, not lecture. If you come down too hard, you risk shutting down the conversation entirely — and that's the last thing you want. Instead, lean into their openness. Say something like:

"So, tell me more about what happened. You know, back in my school days, there were people who tried these things too. It's not new — it's been around forever. Let me tell you this: it's okay to talk about it. The world is full of choices, and what matters is how *we* decide to design our lives."

THE FIRST SECRET: CONNECTION

This approach helps them relax, knowing you're not there to judge but to guide them. You can frame the discussion around family values, gently reminding them, "Life is about weighing what's right and what's wrong. And guess what? I trust you with your MORAL COMPASS. It's yours to use and refine. My role isn't to scold or lecture but to support you as you navigate it."

Reassure them that they can always come to you, no matter what. Say something like, "If something goes wrong, don't hesitate — I'm here to protect and support you. And when things go right, you can count on me to be your loudest cheerleader. You'll never have to face things alone."

Finish with a heartfelt, "I love you, and I trust you." This tells your teen that your bond is stronger than any situation, and they'll feel safe coming to you with anything.

Staying Connected and Communicating

Teenagers are like cats: they crave independence but secretly want to know you're nearby. Maintaining a strong connection helps them feel secure, even as they explore their independence.

Figure 22

1. The Power of Emotional Validation

    Teens want to feel understood — not fixed or judged. When you validate their feelings, you're saying, "I see you, I hear you, and I'm on your team."

- Pro Tip: Respond with empathy. "It sounds like you're really frustrated with your friend. That must be hard to deal with."

2. Mastering Open Communication

    Teens have a knack for opening up at the most inconvenient times (hello, midnight heart-to-hearts!). Stay ready to seize these moments.
    - Practice Active Listening: Resist the urge to interrupt or jump to solutions. "Tell me more about why you feel that way."
    - Create Judgment-Free Zones: Keep the conversation safe for honesty. Avoid responses like, "What were you thinking?!"
    - Be Available: The car ride, bedtime chats, or even making breakfast can be golden opportunities.

Finding Common Ground

Shared activities are like secret backdoors into their world — ways to connect without feeling forced. Ideas for Bonding:

- Cook a meal together (bonus points for their favorite dish).
- Watch their favorite show — even if you don't get the appeal of zombie romances.
- Explore new hobbies, like hiking or painting.

Pro Tip: Treat this time as connection-focused, not correction-focused. No lectures allowed.

The First Secret: Connection

Navigating Conflicts Without Losing Your Cool

Conflict with teens is inevitable, but it doesn't have to be catastrophic. Think of arguments as opportunities to teach life skills like negotiation and empathy.

1. Why Do Teens Push Boundaries?
- Identity Development: They're figuring out who they are, which often means testing the limits.
- Brain Science: Impulse control is still under construction, courtesy of the prefrontal cortex.

2. Strategies for Conflict Resolution
- Stay Calm: Easier said than done, but taking a deep breath before reacting can keep things from escalating.
- Focus on Solutions, Not Blame: How can we make sure this doesn't happen again?"
- Collaborate on Rules: Teens are more likely to respect boundaries they've helped create. "What's a fair curfew for school nights?"

Rebuilding Trust After the Storm

If things go sideways, it's not the end of the world — or your relationship. Trust can be rebuilt, one small step at a time.

- Own Your Mistakes: Teens respect parents who can apologize. "I'm sorry I lost my temper. Let's talk about this calmly."
- Celebrate Progress: Acknowledge when they take responsibility or meet expectations. "I noticed how you managed your time this week — great job keeping up with your homework!"
- Small Trust Deposits: Restore privileges gradually as they demonstrate responsibility.

2.3 THE TEENAGE YEARS (13 TO 18 YEARS)

Turning Conflicts into Connection

According to Dr. Dan Siegel, conflict isn't just inevitable — it's an opportunity to strengthen your relationship. Each argument gives you a chance to understand your teen's perspective and show them that disagreements don't break your bond.

Case Study: Aryan's Grade Drama

Sixteen-year-old Aryan and his mom argued about grades. Aryan felt criticized, while his mom felt he wasn't meeting his potential.

What Mom Did Right

1. Apologized: "I'm sorry I got upset. I just want the best for you."
2. Listened: She learned Aryan was overwhelmed by extracurriculars.
3. Collaborated: Together, they adjusted his schedule to make things manageable.

Outcome: Aryan felt understood, and their relationship grew stronger.

Activity: The "Connection Time Capsule"

Compliment Exchange

- How It Works: Each person takes a moment to share one thing they genuinely appreciate about the other.
- Why It Helps: Builds mutual respect, strengthens bonds, and boosts confidence.
- Write the compliments in a notebook and finally it will become a scrap file.

THE FIRST SECRET: CONNECTION

A simple yet powerful way to create positivity and connection!

The Bigger Picture

Adolescence may feel like a rollercoaster, but it doesn't have to throw your relationship off track. Connection is your anchor — whether it's sharing a laugh, diving into a heartfelt chat, or bonding over late-night pizza runs. Staying calm, practicing empathy, and viewing conflicts as opportunities to grow together will strengthen your bond.

Remember, you're not just raising a teenager — you're shaping a future adult. Every moment of connection today builds a foundation of trust and respect that will last a lifetime.

Parenting teens is messy, magical, and always full of surprises. Lean into the chaos, cherish the connections, and remind yourself — you're doing an incredible job.

2.3.5: Academic and Career Guidance

Teenage years often feel like a whirlwind of grades, extracurriculars, and looming questions about the future. For parents, the challenge is to strike a balance — supporting academic growth and career exploration without piling on the pressure. This chapter is all about fostering curiosity, resilience, and independence as your teen navigates this pivotal time.

2.3 THE TEENAGE YEARS (13 TO 18 YEARS)

Supporting Academic Success Without Overwhelming Pressure

The secret to academic success isn't forcing straight A's — it's nurturing a love for learning and teaching them how to handle challenges with confidence.

1. What Teens Need from You
   Teens face plenty of academic pressure already. Your role is to be their cheerleader, guide, and occasional therapist. Focus on the process, not just the outcome. Celebrate their effort, progress, and persistence. "You've been working so hard on your science project — your dedication is impressive!"

2. Encourage a Growth Mindset
   Always remind your teen that ability isn't fixed — it grows with effort.
   Instead of: "You're just not good at math."
   Try: "Math is tough, but every problem you solve makes you stronger at it."

3. Practical Tips for Academic Support
   - Establish a Routine: Help them create a consistent schedule with time for study, breaks, and fun.
   - Provide an Ideal Workspace: A clutter-free, quiet spot makes all the difference.
   - Encourage Ownership: Resist micromanaging — ask questions instead. "How are you planning to tackle your assignments this week?"
   - Celebrate Efforts: Every small win counts.

THE FIRST SECRET: CONNECTION

4. Ditch the Overwhelming Pressure
   Teens already feel the weight of expectations. Encourage stress management through mindfulness, exercise, or creative outlets.
   Your New Motto: "Grades are just one measure of success — what matters most is how you grow along the way."
   Pro- Tip for Exams – Use these techniques for better results.

Multi-Sensory Learning

Engage multiple senses — like reading, listening, and writing — while studying. This strengthens memory retention and makes learning more engaging.

Memory Palace Technique

Visualize placing information in familiar locations in your mind, like rooms in your house. This method makes recalling complex details easier and more structured.

Exploring Career Interests and Future Planning

Gone are the days when a teen had to choose "doctor, engineer, or lawyer." Today's world offers countless paths, and your teen's job is to explore them.

1. Introduce Career Exploration Without Pressure
   This isn't about locking in a career — it's about figuring out what sparks their interest.

Open-Ended Questions to Start:

- "What's something you'd love to learn more about?"
- "What kinds of problems do you enjoy solving?"

2. Encourage Self-Discovery
   Support your teen in uncovering their strengths and passions.
   - Extracurricular Exploration:
   Suggest activities that align with their interests. Eg.: Love animals? Volunteer at a shelter. Love coding? Join a tech club.
   - Be Open to Change: Their passions might evolve, and that's okay!

3. Strengths-Based Focus
   Donald Clifton's strengths-based approach is a game-changer. Help your teen focus on what they're naturally good at and build on it. E.g.- If they love debating, encourage them to explore public speaking, model UN conferences, or advocacy roles.

4. Simple Steps to Explore Careers
   - Find Mentors: Connect them with professionals in fields they're curious about.
   - Use Online Tools: Career quizzes and job shadowing can open their eyes to possibilities.
   - Reassure Flexibility: Let them know it's okay to change paths. E.g.- "What excites you today might look different in five years — and that's totally normal."

Helping with Decisions: Independence + Guidance

Let your teen take the driver's seat, but don't abandon the passenger role.

- Decision Frameworks: Teach them to weigh pros and cons. E.g.- "Joining the swim team sounds fun, but how will it fit with your study schedule?"

THE FIRST SECRET: CONNECTION

- One Size Doesn't Fit All: Whether they're college-bound, trade school-bound, or ready for something else, their journey is unique and valid.

Unique Way to Access It: The "Passion Palette"

Here's a fun way to help your teen connect the dots between their interests and potential careers.

What You'll Need

- A large sheet of paper or digital tool.
- Markers, pens, or a design app.

Steps

1. Divide the Palette: Sections like "Hobbies," "Skills to Build," and "Dream Careers."
2. Add Their Ideas: Encourage creativity.
3. Reflect and Update: Revisit the palette regularly to track how their interests evolve.

Case Study: Meera's Spark

Meera, 15, felt uninspired by her parents' focus on grades. After an honest chat, they discovered her passion for art and technology.

- Together, they explored graphic design.
- Meera joined a design club and took an online course.
- Her parents celebrated her effort instead of focusing solely on results.

Meera found confidence in her skills and excitement for her future.

2.3 THE TEENAGE YEARS (13 TO 18 YEARS)

Activity: Career Exploration Map

Objective: Help your teen visualize how their passions can connect to potential careers.

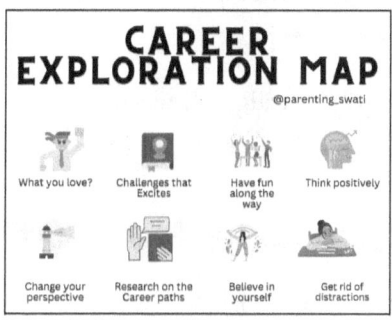

Figure 23

Steps

1. Brainstorm Interests:
   - *What do they love doing?*
   - *What challenges excite them?*
2. Match Interests to Careers:
   - *Use career quizzes or research to find related fields.*
3. Set a Goal:
   - *Explore one field through shadowing, research, or a related project.*

Guiding your teen through academics and career exploration isn't just about helping them prepare for the future — it's about giving them the confidence to own it. Celebrate their efforts, cheer their discoveries, and trust their journey. You've got this! 🚀

THE FIRST SECRET: CONNECTION

The Bigger Picture

Academic and career guidance is about more than grades and job titles — it's about fostering curiosity, resilience, and self-discovery. Your role isn't to map out their path but to hand them the compass and encourage them to explore.

Remember: Life isn't a straight line, and every step — whether forward or sideways — is part of the journey.

2.3.6: Social Dynamics and Peer Influence

Teenage friendships can feel like the center of the universe — bringing drama, joy, and plenty of life lessons along the way. As parents, your role shifts from orchestrating playdates to helping your teen navigate the often-murky waters of social dynamics. While you can't pick their friends or prevent every heartbreak, you can equip them with the skills and confidence to build meaningful relationships and resist peer pressure.

Helping Teens Build Healthy Friendships

1. Why Friendships Matter
   For teens, friendships are more than just fun — they're a cornerstone of emotional and social development.
   - The Bright Side: Positive friendships foster empathy, trust, and self-esteem.
   - The Dark Side: Toxic relationships can lead to stress, insecurity, or exposure to risky behavior.

2. Be the Behind-the-Scenes Support
   Your teen might not want you to tag along to hangouts, but they do need your guidance.

- Model Healthy Relationships: Demonstrate kindness, respect, and boundary-setting in your own interactions.
- Open the Door for Conversation:
  - *Ask: "What do you love most about your friends?"*
  - *Reflect: "It's great that they make you laugh. What else do you value in a friendship?"*

3. Handling Friendship Conflicts

    Friendship spats are inevitable. Help your teen navigate them with empathy and poise.
    - Teach Them to Speak Up: Encourage "I" statements for clear, constructive communication:
      - *"I felt hurt when you canceled our plans last minute."*
    - Normalize Disagreements: Remind them that healthy conflict can strengthen relationships when resolved respectfully.

Addressing Peer Pressure with Confidence

1. The Power of Peers

    The teen years are a balancing act between individuality and the need for acceptance. Peer pressure — both positive and negative — can influence decisions, from trying new activities to risky behaviors. Peers can help you become Starbucks or local coffee, because when you are with the right people only then you grow and evolve as a person. So, choosing the right friend is very crucial.

2. Building a Solid Foundation of Confidence

    A confident teen is less likely to feel pressured into something they don't want to do.

- Celebrate Their Strengths: "I love how you always stand up for your friends. That takes courage."
- Encourage Independence: Give them space to make decisions and learn from mistakes.
- Model Self-Talk: Replace self-doubt with affirmations: "I can handle this" or "I know what's right for me."

3. How to Handle Peer Pressure

   Equip your teen with tools to resist pressure gracefully.
   - Teach Refusal Skills: Practice simple, confident responses like:
     - *"No thanks, I'm not into that."*
     - *"I've got other plans."*
   - Role-Play Scenarios: Work through real-life situations together:
     - *"What would you say if someone dared you to skip class?"*
   - Encourage Critical Thinking: Help them evaluate the consequences of actions:
     - *"How would this choice affect you tomorrow? Next week?"*

The Friendship Filter: A Tool for Healthy Relationships

Help your teen evaluate friendships with these three simple questions:

1. Does this friend make me feel good about myself?
2. Can I trust them with my thoughts and feelings?
3. Do they respect my boundaries?
   - Pro Tip: Revisit the Friendship Filter during tough moments to encourage reflection without judgment.

2.3 THE TEENAGE YEARS (13 TO 18 YEARS)

Case Study: Aarav Finds His People

Fourteen-year-old Aarav felt pressured to skip school by friends who often teased him for being "too serious."

- Parent Intervention: Aarav's parents asked, "How do you feel after spending time with this group?" Realizing he felt anxious, Aarav explored other activities.
- The Switch: He joined his school's robotics club and found friends who shared his love of technology.
- The Result: Aarav built confidence and discovered the joy of supportive friendships.

Psychological Insights to Guide You

Erik Erikson's "Identity vs. Role Confusion": Friendships play a significant role in shaping teens' identities. Positive relationships help teens discover who they are, while negative influences may lead to self-doubt.

Albert Bandura's Social Learning Theory: Teens imitate behaviors they observe in peers and role models. Positive examples can inspire good habits and healthy decision-making.

Practical Tips for Parents

1. Be Involved Without Hovering: Attend events and get to know your teenager's friends casually. However, respect their privacy.
2. Emphasize Respect: Make it clear that all relationships should be based on mutual respect — no exceptions.

3. **Promote Diverse Friendships:** Encourage your teen to join clubs, sports, or volunteer opportunities to meet different people.

Activity: The Friendship Map: Peer Influence Worksheet

Objective: Help your teen reflect on their social circle and identify supportive relationships.

Steps

- *Describe the situation with your peers.*
- *List the options you had at that moment.*
- *Reflect on your emotions during and after the situation.*
- *Plan a response for similar situations in the future.*

Encourage thoughtful decision-making and self-awareness!

The Bigger Picture

Teen friendships are like the practice field for adult relationships. By helping your teen build self-confidence, set healthy boundaries, and recognize positive connections, you're equipping them to navigate the ups and downs of their social world with resilience.

Your role isn't to control every friendship or shield them from every hurt, but to give them the tools to choose relationships that uplift them — and walk away from the ones that don't.

Navigating teen social dynamics may feel like a rollercoaster, but it's also an opportunity for growth, bonding, and even a few laughs. With your steady guidance, your teen will learn to embrace friendships that bring out the best in them and carry those lessons into adulthood.

2.3.7: Screen Time, Social Media, and Digital Boundaries

Screens are everywhere in the teenage years, from late-night TikTok binges to group chats that buzz around the clock. For teens, technology can feel like both a lifeline and a trap. For parents? It's a tightrope walk — balancing the benefits of digital connection with the risks of overuse. But don't worry; with a little humor and a lot of patience, you can help your teen develop a healthy relationship with technology.

Understanding the Teen Relationship with Technology

1. A Tool for Connection: For teens, social media isn't just an app; it's their social hub. From group chats to Snapchat streaks, it helps them bond, share, and express themselves.
2. The Dopamine Loop: Likes, comments, and notifications trigger dopamine — the brain's feel-good chemical. Apps are designed to keep your teen scrolling, but explaining this can help them unplug.
   Parent Tip: "That endless scrolling you're doing? It's not your fault — your brain loves that dopamine hit!"
3. Mirror Neurons at Play: Teens mimic behaviors they observe — including yours. Modelling balanced screen habits can go a long way in teaching them to do the same.

The Role of Video Games in Teens

Video games are a major part of many teenagers' lives, with both positive and negative impacts. Understanding their role can help parents guide teens toward healthy gaming habits.

THE FIRST SECRET: CONNECTION

Positive Impacts

1. Cognitive Benefits: Improves problem-solving, strategic thinking, and hand-eye coordination. Some games enhance creativity and critical thinking.
2. Social Interaction: Multiplayer games foster teamwork and collaboration with peers. Online communities can create a sense of belonging.
3. Stress Relief: Gaming provides an outlet for relaxation and a break from academic pressures.

Negative Impacts

1. Addiction Risks: Excessive gaming can lead to neglect of responsibilities, sleep deprivation, and poor academic performance.
2. Aggression: Prolonged exposure to violent games may desensitize teens to aggression or increase irritability in some cases.
3. Physical Health: Sedentary habits contribute to obesity, poor posture, and eye strain.
4. Social Withdrawal: Over-reliance on virtual interactions may reduce face-to-face communication skills.

Tips for Healthy Gaming Habits

1. Set Time Limits: Encourage balance with academics, hobbies, and physical activities.
2. Choose Appropriate Games: Opt for age-appropriate, non-violent, and educational games.
3. Encourage Breaks: Use timers to prevent prolonged gaming sessions.

2.3 THE TEENAGE YEARS (13 TO 18 YEARS)

4. Promote Offline Socializing: Encourage activities like sports or group projects to balance online interactions.
5. Family Engagement: Play games together to monitor content and build stronger bonds.

Video games can be a valuable tool for learning and socializing when used mindfully. However, balance is key — moderation and guidance ensure teens enjoy the benefits of gaming without its potential downsides.

Unique Strategies for Digital Boundaries

1. The Digital Diet: Compare screen time to food: balance "tech nourishment" (e.g., coding, educational content) with "tech treats" (e.g., Netflix or gaming).
   - Activity: Create a "digital plate" with your teen, dividing their screen time into categories of learning, creativity, and leisure.
2. Pause, Reflect, Act: Encourage teens to pause before posting or reacting online.
   - Reflect: Does this post align with who I want to be?
   - Act Mindfully: Take a moment to think before clicking.
3. The Social-Media Mirror: Ask your teen: "What does your online presence say about you? Does it reflect your true self or just what you think people want to see?"

Protecting Teens from Digital Risks

Common Challenges

1. Cyberbullying: Results in anxiety, depression, and social withdrawal.

2. Overuse: Too much screen time can lead to mental health issues like anxiety and feelings of inadequacy.
3. FOMO (Fear of Missing Out): The curated perfection of social media can make teens feel left out or not good enough.
4. Social Media: Because of social- media, teens seek validation from unknown people. The number of likes tells them if they are good looking or not. They have become people pleasers forgetting about their true self. Their self-confidence goes for a ride which leads to self-harm and self-doubt.

Practical Strategies

1. Family Digital Agreement: Collaborate with your teen to set boundaries:
    - *Screen-free meals.*
    - *No phones an hour before bed.*
2. Teach Media Literacy: Encourage teens to question content authenticity:
    - *"Do you think that photo was filtered or edited?"*
3. Empower Self-Curation: Teach them to "mute" or "unfollow" accounts that negatively impact their mood.
4. Monitor Transparently: Use parental controls openly, emphasizing safety over surveillance.
    - *"This isn't about spying — it's about keeping you safe."*

Balancing Screen Time and Real Life

1. Model Healthy Tech Use: Teens are experts at spotting hypocrisy, so practice what you preach. Narrate your choices: "I'm turning off my phone to enjoy dinner with you."

2.3 THE TEENAGE YEARS (13 TO 18 YEARS)

2. Encourage Offline Hobbies: Help them discover screen-free passions: sports, art, volunteering — whatever lights them up.
3. Recognize Positive Tech Use: When they use technology creatively — whether coding, creating digital art, or making videos — celebrate it! "Your video editing skills are awesome. Maybe this could be a future career!"

Case Study: From Overuse to Balance

Meet Meera: Fourteen-year-old Meera spent hours scrolling through Instagram, comparing herself to others and feeling left out.

- *Pause, Reflect, Act: Helped Meera think about why she posted and how it aligned with her values.*
- *Channel Creativity: Signed her up for a photography class to turn her scrolling into inspiration.*
- *Digital Diet: Together, they created a balance between productive and leisure screen time.*

Finally, Meera began viewing social media as a platform for self-expression rather than validation.

Activity: The Digital Reset Challenge

Purpose: Help your teen develop healthier tech habits through reflection and small changes.

THE FIRST SECRET: CONNECTION

DIGITAL RESET CHALLENGE @parenting_swati	
Today's Screen Time	
Junk Scrolling	
Hobby Time	
Playing Outdoor	
Mood of the Day	
Read a Book	
Chit Chat Family Time	
Activity Enjoyed Most	

Figure 24

Steps

1. Digital Audit: Review their daily screen time together. Discuss what they enjoy and what drains their energy.
2. Set Goals: Reduce "junk scrolling" by 20 minutes a day. Replace it with activities like reading, hobbies, or physical exercise.
3. Reflect Weekly: Discuss how these changes impacted their mood, focus, and energy.

The Bigger Picture

Screen time itself isn't the problem — it's how your teen engages with it that makes all the difference. By teaching thoughtful tech habits, keeping communication open, and establishing boundaries, you're empowering your teen to thrive in the digital world with confidence and purpose.

You're not just overseeing their TikTok or Snapchat streaks; you're helping them find a balance between the virtual and real worlds. With your guidance, they'll discover how to use technology as a tool for creativity, connection, and learning, rather than a measure of self-worth.

Parenting in the digital age comes with its challenges, but you're not navigating this alone. Together, you and your teen can create a tech life that's balanced, intentional, and full of humor and heart.

2.3.8: Physical and Mental Health

Teenagers are a whirlwind of growth and energy — both physically and emotionally. They're navigating hormones, identity shifts, academic challenges, and TikTok dances (sometimes all at once). Amid this chaos, building healthy habits for sleep, nutrition, and mental well-being becomes essential. The good news? With a dash of understanding and a sprinkle of humor, you can help your teen thrive.

Promoting Healthy Habits: Sleep, Nutrition, and Wellness

Why Teens Need More Sleep (and Why They Never Seem to Get It)

Sleep-deprived teens are almost a universal phenomenon. Despite needing 8–10 hours a night, many teens function on much less due to biology, school schedules, and Netflix cliffhangers.

1. Teen Brain Science
   - *Delayed Sleep Phase Syndrome: Their body clocks naturally shift, making them night owls who dread mornings.*
   - *Brain Development: Sleep fuels growth in the prefrontal cortex (hello, decision-making!) and emotional regulation.*

THE FIRST SECRET: CONNECTION

Without enough, expect grumpiness, memory lapses, and a fridge emptied at 2 AM.

2. How You Can Help
   - *Encourage Consistency: Help them stick to regular sleep and wake times (yes, even on weekends).*
   - *Golden Hour Wind-Down: Swap screens for journaling, reading, or calming music an hour before bed.*
   - *Advocate for Later School Starts: Team up with schools to align schedules with teen biology.*

Nutrition: Fueling Growth and Mood

Teenagers grow faster than bamboo shoots, and they need the right fuel for this stage. Balanced nutrition isn't just about strong bones — it's also about keeping their mood swings in check.

1. What to Serve
   - *Protein & Whole Grains: For sustained energy. Think eggs, lentils, or a hearty quinoa salad.*
   - *Healthy Fats: Avocados, nuts, and olive oil for brain power.*
   - *Fruits & Veggies: No bribes required if you get creative with smoothies or fun salads.*

2. Family Meals Matter
   - *Sit-down dinners aren't just for eating — they're prime time for connection. Use this time to chat about their day (and stealthily check if they ate their greens).*

3. The Junk Food Talk
   - *Rather than banning treats, discuss moderation: "How does eating this make you feel later? Does it fuel you or slow you down?"*

- *Eating French Fries Worse Than Smoking Cigarettes? French fries are high in trans fats, refined carbs, and sodium. When fried at high temperatures, they produce acrylamide, a chemical linked to cancer risks. Honestly, we don't really know how many times the same oil has been used for frying. Regular consumption can lead to obesity, heart disease, high blood pressure, and diabetes.*

Supporting Mental Health: Tackling Stress and Mood Swings

Common Mental Health Challenges

1. Stress and Anxiety: Balancing academics, friendships, and "what-am-I-going-to-do-with-my-life" thoughts can be overwhelming.
2. Body Image Pressures: Social media adds a layer of scrutiny that even adults struggle with.
3. Depression: Look for signs like withdrawal, persistent sadness, or a sudden drop in grades or interests.

How You Can Help?

1. Open the Door for Conversations
   - *Notice changes: "You've seemed quieter lately. Want to talk about it?"*
   - *Avoid rushing to solutions — sometimes, just listening is enough.*

2. Model Emotional Resilience
   - *Show them how you handle stress: "Today was tough, so I'm going for a walk to clear my head."*
   - *Teach simple coping tools like deep breathing or visualization.*

3. When to Seek Help
   - *Professional counseling is a strength, not a last resort. Remind them it's okay to need help.*

The Golden Hour: Prioritizing Well-Being Before Bed

This pre-sleep window is a magical time for reflection, connection, and calm.

Ideas for the Golden Hour

1. Gratitude Journaling: Encourage them to jot down three things they're thankful for each night. Positivity can reduce stress and anxiety.
2. Relaxation Techniques: Try guided deep breathing: inhale for 4 seconds, hold for 7, exhale for 8.
3. Story Sharing: Swap a funny or meaningful memory from your day — it shows them you're human, too.
4. Quiet Time Together: Sit in comfortable silence. Sometimes, just being there speaks volumes.

Unique Psychological Concepts

1. Maslow's Hierarchy of Needs: Teens can't focus on academic or personal goals if their basic needs — sleep, nutrition, and emotional security — aren't met.
2. The "Window of Opportunity": This phase of heightened brain plasticity is perfect for instilling lifelong resilience and self-care habits.

2.3 THE TEENAGE YEARS (13 TO 18 YEARS)

Case Study: Riya's Sleep Rescue

The Challenge: Fifteen-year-old Riya stayed up scrolling on her phone, resulting in grumpiness, poor grades, and a daily game of "Why won't you wake up?"

1. Banned screens an hour before bed.
2. Replaced late-night scrolling with journaling and relaxing music.
3. Started nightly chats to reconnect and unwind together.

Riya's sleep improved, her mood stabilized, and she started acing her exams without those post-lunch naps.

Activity: The Wellness Wheel

Objective: Help your teen assess and balance their health habits.

Figure 25

Steps

1. Draw a Circle: Divide it into sections - Sleep, Nutrition, Exercise, Relaxation, and Connections.

2. Rate Each Area: Ask your teen to rate their satisfaction in each section from 1–10.
3. Set Goals: Pick one area to improve. For example:
   - *Low score in "Sleep"? Goal: No screens after 9 PM.*
   - *Low score in "Exercise"? Goal: Walk 20 minutes daily.*
4. Reflect Weekly: Revisit the wheel and celebrate progress.

The Bigger Picture

Teen health isn't just about salads and sleep schedules — it's about building a foundation of balance, resilience, and self-care. By keeping communication open, leading by example, and offering support when they need it, you're giving your teen the tools for lifelong wellness.

Remember, progress always beats perfection. Celebrate every small win, whether it's an extra veggie on their plate or an earlier bedtime.

Helping your teen cultivate healthy habits now isn't just about their present — it's about setting them up for a future of strength and well-being. And who knows? You might even pick up some healthier habits for yourself along the way!

2.3.9: Sexuality, Relationships, and Safety

Teenage years bring with them the thrill of first crushes, the confusion of mixed signals, and the all-important lessons in love, respect, and boundaries. While these topics may seem daunting to tackle, your guidance can be a steady compass in your teen's journey toward understanding relationships and their own sexuality. Think of these conversations as opportunities to foster

2.3 THE TEENAGE YEARS (13 TO 18 YEARS)

trust, empower their decision-making, and help them navigate these exciting yet complex years.

The Importance of Open and Honest Communication

Why It Matters?

1. Trust Is Key: Teens are more likely to share their thoughts and ask for advice when they know you're approachable.
2. Delay and Discourage Risky Behavior: Research shows that honest conversations can encourage teens to make safer, more thoughtful choices.
3. Building Values: You're shaping how they think about respect, love, and self-worth — powerful lessons for a lifetime.

How to Navigate the Talk

1. Start Small and Early: You don't need to dive into the birds and the bees right away. Let conversations evolve naturally with your teen's maturity.
   - Ages 13–15: Focus on emotional connections and boundaries. *Example*: "It's okay to feel attracted to someone. What's most important is treating them — and yourself — with kindness and respect."
   - Ages 16–18: Expand to include sexual health, consent, and long-term relationship dynamics. *Example*: "When you're in a relationship, feeling safe and respected is key. What does that look like to you?"
2. Consent Is Non-Negotiable
   Teach your teen that consent is the foundation of all healthy relationships, and it applies to everyday interactions too.

- **Daily Practice:** Encourage asking for permission and respecting answers, even in small scenarios: *Example*: "Can I borrow your headphones?" or "Do you want a hug?"
- **Handling Rejection Gracefully:** Model and teach how to accept "no" without resentment.

3. Focus on Emotional Well-Being
   Relationships can be a rollercoaster of emotions — rejection, infatuation, and jealousy included. Be their anchor. *Example*: "It's okay to feel hurt when things don't work out. Let's talk about what happened and how you can process it."

Equipping Teens with Knowledge and Confidence

Comprehensive Sexuality Education

Accurate information empowers teens to make safe, informed choices.

- Talk About Prevention: Explain birth control, STIs, and health check-ups.

Example: "Condoms are important for protection, not just against pregnancy but also STIs. Want me to show you how they work?"

- Encourage Regular Health Check-Ups: Normalize discussions about health, including gynaecological or urological visits.

Teach Healthy Relationship Skills

Help your teen recognize the hallmarks of healthy and toxic relationships.

- Healthy Dynamics: Communication, respect, trust, and shared values.

Example: "What do you appreciate most in your closest friends? Those qualities should also be in a romantic partner."

- Spotting Red Flags: Jealousy, manipulation, or pressure to do things they're uncomfortable with.

Example: "If someone makes you feel guilty for setting a boundary, that's a sign they may not respect you fully."

Digital Safety and Boundaries

Navigating Online Relationships with social media and texting at the forefront of teen relationships, it's essential to teach digital literacy and boundaries.

1. Think Before Sharing: *Example*: "Once something is online, it's hard to take back. Always ask yourself how you'd feel if someone else saw it."
2. Risks of Sexting: Be upfront about the legal and emotional consequences. *Example:* "If someone pressures you for pictures, it's okay to say no — and I'll always back you up."
3. Curate Online Spaces: Teach teens to use tools like blocking or muting to maintain a positive digital environment.

Inclusion and Respect for Diversity

LGBTQ+ Inclusion

Celebrate and normalize all identities and orientations. *Example*: "Whoever you're attracted to, what matters most is that you're treated with respect and kindness."

Cultural and Religious Perspectives

Navigate differing family or societal values with empathy and open-mindedness. *Example*: "Our beliefs shape how we view relationships. It's okay to ask questions and figure out what feels right for you."

Case Study: A Relationship Talk That Built Trust

Sixteen-year-old Ravi hesitated to talk about his relationship, fearing judgment from his parents. Over dinner, his parents casually asked, "What do you think makes a great partner?" Ravi felt encouraged to share his thoughts, opening the door for deeper conversations about boundaries, respect, and consent over time.

Activity: The Relationship Bar graph

Objective: Help your teen reflect on what makes healthy relationships.

Steps

1. Create a Bar Graph: Draw an X and Y axis. X-axis has 6 parts- Trust, Respect, Communication, Fun, Support, and Independence.
2. Y axis will have Relationship rate: Ask your teen to rate their friendships or romantic relationships in each area from 1–10.
3. Discuss: Use their responses to start a conversation. "What's working well in these relationships? What could improve?"

This simple activity reinforces the values of healthy relationships while giving your teen a chance to reflect and share.

The Bigger Picture

Discussing sexuality and relationships isn't about one "big talk" — it's an ongoing dialogue that grows with your teen. By staying approachable, providing accurate information, and fostering a values-based approach, you're equipping your teen to navigate love, intimacy, and safety with confidence.

Your guidance now will shape how they view relationships for the rest of their lives — what a privilege and responsibility!

2.3.10: Fostering Creativity and Passion Projects

Adolescence is a whirlwind of growth, self-discovery, and possibility. It's the perfect time to encourage creativity and passion, as hobbies provide teens with a unique outlet for expression, a sense of purpose, and skills they'll carry into adulthood. Your role as a parent is to nurture their curiosity, support their exploration, and cheer them on as they dive into the pursuits that make their hearts sing.

Why Creativity and Passions Matter

1. Identity Formation
   Erik Erikson described adolescence as the "Identity vs. Role Confusion" stage, where teens explore who they are. Creative pursuits and hobbies allow them to try on different "hats" and discover what truly resonates.
2. Emotional Well-Being
   Art, music, sports, or even tinkering with gadgets can be powerful stress-busters. These activities offer teens a healthy way to process emotions and recharge.

3. Skill Development
   From perseverance to teamwork, hobbies teach essential life skills. Whether they're painting a masterpiece or perfecting their free throw, every effort builds confidence and resilience.

Encouraging Hobbies and Interests

1. Provide Exposure to Diverse Activities
   Teens won't know what they love until they try it. Expose them to a variety of activities — gardening, photography, coding, baking, theater, or sports.
   - Pro Tip: Think outside the box! If they're obsessed with gaming, introduce them to game design or animation.
2. Listen and Observe
   Pay attention to where your teen naturally gravitates. *Example*: If your teen spends hours experimenting in the kitchen, surprise them with a cookbook or enroll them in a cooking workshop.
3. Offer Encouragement Without Pressure
   Support their passions without turning them into obligations.
   - *Instead of*: "You should sign up for that competition!"
   - *Try*: "You seem to really enjoy playing the piano. What do you like most about it?"

Balancing Academics and Personal Pursuits

1. Teach Time Management: Help your teen create a balanced schedule that allows for academics, hobbies, and downtime.
   - Use planners or apps to prioritize tasks and set realistic goals.

2. Frame Interests as Assets: Show them how their passions can complement their academics and future goals. *Example*: "Your love for robotics could lead to a great career in engineering!"
3. Encourage Downtime: Creativity thrives in unstructured moments. Ensure they have time to relax, daydream, or experiment without an agenda.

The Magic of Passion Projects

Passion projects are self-directed endeavors where teens explore a topic they love. Think of them as a deep dive into curiosity and creativity.

- Examples: Writing a novel, starting a YouTube channel, building a DIY greenhouse, or organizing a neighborhood cleanup.

How to Support Passion Projects
- Define Goals: Help them break their project into manageable steps. *Example*: "Let's map out what you'll need to film your short movie."
- Provide Resources: Support their efforts with tools, connections, or even just your time. *Example*: Offer to drive them to the library or help them find tutorials online.
- Celebrate Progress: Acknowledge their milestones, no matter how small.

The Science of Creativity

1. Divergent Thinking

THE FIRST SECRET: CONNECTION

Creative pursuits help teens develop divergent thinking — the ability to generate multiple solutions to a problem, a skill that psychologist J.P. Guilford emphasized.

2. Flow State
Introduced by Mihaly Csikszentmihalyi, the concept of "flow" describes being fully immersed in an activity. Teens often experience this blissful focus while working on hobbies or passion projects, which enhances satisfaction and productivity.

Case Study: Suhani's Solar-Powered Dream

Scenario: Fourteen-year-old Suhani loved tinkering with gadgets but felt overwhelmed balancing school and hobbies.

Parent's Approach:
1. They set aside Saturdays as "Tinker Time" for Suhani to focus on his passion.
2. With their encouragement, Suhani built a solar-powered phone charger, which she presented at his school's science fair.
3. They celebrated her progress, regardless of the outcome.

Outcome: Suhani gained confidence, developed time-management skills, and discovered a sense of accomplishment.

Activity: The Passion Pie chart

Objective: Help your teen identify and pursue their passions.

1. Draw It: Create a pie chart titled *"What I Love"* and jot down interests and hobbies in each slice.
2. Find Patterns: Spot the biggest slice — it's likely their top passion.
3. Set Goals: Outline small steps to explore this passion further.

4. Reflect: Check progress regularly and celebrate wins.

A simple way to turn interests into meaningful growth!

The Bigger Picture

Teen health isn't just about salads and sleep schedules — it's about building a foundation of balance, resilience, and self-care. By keeping communication open, leading by example, and offering support when they need it, you're giving your teen the tools for lifelong wellness.

Remember, progress always beats perfection. Celebrate every small win, whether it's an extra veggie on their plate or an earlier bedtime.

Helping your teen cultivate healthy habits now isn't just about their present — it's about setting them up for a future of strength and well-being. And who knows? You might even pick up some healthier habits for yourself along the way!

2.3.11: Preparing for Adulthood

Adolescence is more than a bridge between childhood and adulthood — it's a transformative journey filled with discovery, challenges, and growth. As your teen steps closer to independence, your role as a parent evolves, moving from hands-on guide to a trusted mentor. This stage is not just about preparing them for the world but also about celebrating the bond you've built with them and the incredible person they're becoming.

THE FIRST SECRET: CONNECTION

The Shift: From Parent to Mentor

Parenting a teenager is like tending a garden. The groundwork you've laid during their earlier years has set the stage for their growth, and now it's time to step back, offer support, and let them bloom.

Why Mentorship Matters

- Autonomy: Teens thrive when they feel trusted to make decisions, even if they occasionally stumble.
- Collaboration: Involving your teen in conversations about their goals and challenges fosters mutual respect.

Practical Tips for Mentorship

- Encourage Ownership: "What's your plan for balancing school and your part-time job?"
- Model Confidence in Their Abilities: "I trust you'll handle this; let me know if you need advice."

Equipping Teens with Life Skills

Adulthood requires more than academic knowledge — it's about mastering practical skills and emotional resilience.

Life Skills Every Teen Needs

1. Financial Literacy: Teach Basics: Budgeting, saving, and understanding credit.
    - *Activity: Open a savings account together and set short-term savings goals.*

2. Problem-Solving: Encourage Reflection: "What worked in solving this issue? What would you change next time?"
   - *Activity: Role-play scenarios, like handling a customer service issue or planning a budget-friendly trip.*
3. Everyday Independence: Skills to Master: Cooking, laundry, and basic home maintenance.
   - *Activity: Turn dinner prep into a weekly family event where everyone learns a new recipe.*

Preparing for the Big Leap

As teens prepare to leave high school, whether they're headed for college, a career, or something else entirely, they need guidance to navigate this transition.

Exploring Future Paths

- For College-Bound Teens: Help with applications, scholarships, and prepare for life away from home.
- For Career-Driven Teens: Explore internships, trade schools, or entrepreneurial opportunities.
- For Uncertain Teens: Emphasize exploration and adaptability: "Your path doesn't have to be linear. It's okay to try different things."

MUST DO: Goal-Setting Exercise

- Create a vision board with short- and long-term aspirations.
- Break goals into actionable steps and celebrate progress along the way.

THE FIRST SECRET: CONNECTION

Building Emotional Resilience

Preparing for adulthood isn't just about practical skills — it's about helping your teen develop the emotional tools they'll need to navigate life's highs and lows.

Fostering Emotional Independence

- Teach Self-Reflection: Encourage journaling or mindfulness to help them process emotions.
- Normalize Asking for Help: Remind them that seeking support is a strength, not a weakness.

Modeling Resilience

- Share your own coping strategies: "When I'm overwhelmed, I take a walk to clear my head."

Celebrating the Journey

Preparing for adulthood isn't just about what's ahead — it's also a moment to reflect on how far you've both come.

Recognizing Growth

- For Your Teen: Celebrate their milestones — big and small. "I'm so proud of how you handled that tough situation with maturity."
- For Yourself: Acknowledge your evolution as a parent. "I've learned so much about patience, adaptability, and unconditional love through this journey."

2.3 THE TEENAGE YEARS (13 TO 18 YEARS)

Looking Ahead: A Lifelong Bond

Your relationship with your teen is evolving, but it's far from over. While they may no longer need your guidance for everyday decisions, they'll always look to you for support, wisdom, and love.

- From Protector to Partner: Be their sounding board and cheerleader as they navigate early adulthood.
- Celebrate Their Autonomy: Let them take the lead while reminding them that you're always there when needed.

A Parting Message

Parenting is about showing up, learning alongside your teen, and loving them through every phase. As they step into adulthood, know that the values, skills, and resilience you've nurtured will guide them, even when they're out of sight.

Cherish the moments you've shared and look forward to the memories yet to come. Together, you've built a foundation of trust and love that will remain steady no matter where life takes them.

Here's to the incredible journey you've shared — and the bright future ahead.

Activity: "Life Skills Checklist"

Objective: Help teens assess and build essential life skills.

Steps:
1. Create a checklist with categories such as:
   o *Cooking a basic meal.*

LIFE SKILLS CHECKLIST
@parenting_swati
- ☐ Cooking Basic Meal
- ☐ Managing a Budget
- ☐ Writing a Letter / Email
- ☐ Taking Care of Chores
- ☐ Reading Challenge

Figure 26

THE FIRST SECRET: CONNECTION

- *Managing a budget.*
- *Writing a professional email.*
- *Scheduling and time management.*

2. Encourage them to rate their confidence level in each skill (1–5).
3. Collaborate on a plan to improve weaker areas. You can check this checklist every week to see how many things you have ticked.

The Bigger Picture: Teen Health and Wellness

Teen health isn't just about salads and sleep schedules — it's about building a foundation of balance, resilience, and self-care. By keeping communication open, leading by example, and offering support when they need it, you're giving your teen the tools for lifelong wellness. Celebrate every small win, whether it's an extra veggie on their plate or an earlier bedtime.

Helping your teen cultivate healthy habits now isn't just about their present — it's about setting them up for a future of strength and well-being. And who knows? You might even pick up some healthier habits for yourself along the way!

Parenting through adolescence is a remarkable chapter — one filled with love, learning, and transformation. As this stage draws to a close, celebrate all that you and your teen have accomplished. The road ahead is full of promise, and together, you've built a bond that will last a lifetime. Now let's move ahead to the "Second Secret".

Section 1
What is Parenting

Section 2
The First Secret
Connection

2.1
Foundation Years
1 - 5 Years

2.2
Middle Childhood
6 - 12 Years

2.3
Teenage Years
13 - 18 Years

Section 3
The Second Secret
Care

YOU ARE HERE

Section 4
The Third Secret
Celebrate

Section 5
Parent Survival Kit
50+ Activities

Your Parenting Journey

SECTION 3

THE SECOND SECRET: CARE

Is Self-Care Selfish or Self-Ishq?

Are You Not Enough?

As a parent, do you feel you are not enough?

Parenting is showing up with love, patience, and an open heart — not about being perfect. This book will remind you of your incredible strength, even on the days when it feels like you're just holding it together. Together, we'll unpack the challenges, celebrate your wins, and create a home where you and your children can thrive.

You're not just raising a child — you're shaping a person. You're building a legacy of love, resilience, and connection. Along the way, you'll also rediscover yourself — your strengths, your creativity, and the endless capacity of your heart.

When you take a wrong turn on Google Maps, it doesn't yell at you or lose its temper. Instead, it calmly recalculates and shows you a new route to your destination. Sure, it might take a little longer or send you on a different path, but you'll still get there.

Parenting is a lot like that. When kids make mistakes or take a wrong turn in life, there's no need to scream or scold. Instead, guide them gently, show them the next steps, and help them get back on track.

Remember this, let's embrace the challenges, celebrate parenthood, and, most importantly, enjoy the ride. I am your GPS guide in your parenting journey because when you know better you do better.

Let's walk this path together. The world is waiting for the best version of you and your family.

Today, my mission is clear: to help parents find joy in parenting, build strong bonds with their children, lead fulfilled family lives, and achieve financial freedom. Writing this book is an act of love and gratitude. To everyone who trusts me and joins my community, you are my family. And now, if you're reading this book, you are part of my family too. I am here to serve you.

Parenting isn't a sprint; it's a lifelong marathon. And like any marathon, pacing yourself is key. This chapter is about embracing self-care without guilt and mastering communication and emotional regulation as tools for a smoother, more joyful parenting journey. Together, these practices not only nurture your well-being but also strengthen the bond you share with children.

Dear Parent,

THE SECOND SECRET: CARE

This chapter is about you. Not the carpooling, multi-tasking, always-on version of you, but the one underneath it all — the you who dreams, who feels, who gives so much without pausing to refill.

Parenting is one of life's most profound roles, yet it often comes with an unspoken rule: sacrifice. But here's the truth — it's not selfish to take care of yourself. It's an act of love. Because when you nurture your own well-being, you nurture the very foundation of children's world.

The Heart of Self-Care: Why You Matter

DON'T CUT YOUR WINGS when the child is born- whether working parent or staying at home parent decision is yours and no one else can take it for you.

Children see you not just as a caregiver but as their compass. Your energy, patience, and joy shape their sense of security and happiness. When you care for yourself, you model resilience, self-respect, and love — all the things you hope to teach them.

Why Self-Care Matters

- **You Are Their Anchor:** A calm, balanced you creates a steady, nurturing environment for their growth.
- **You Are Their Mirror:** They learn how to navigate emotions by watching you care for yourself.
- **Brain Chemistry Bonus:** Taking care of yourself boosts your "happy hormones" — dopamine, serotonin, oxytocin, and endorphins — helping you stay energized and resilient.

THE SECOND SECRET: CARE

PRO TIP: Have and live a full life… Find your nanny or delegate the task to someone whom you trust.

Self-Care is Self-Ishq, Not Selfish

Small Acts of Self-Love: Building Your Sanctuary

Self-care doesn't require grand gestures. It's the small, intentional moments that remind you of who you are.

Figure 27

How to Stay Balanced?

1. The 4D Method for Time Management:
   - *Delete: Eliminate tasks that aren't necessary.*
   - *Delegate: Share responsibilities with family or friends.*
   - *Defy: Challenge perfectionism — done is better than perfect.*
   - *Do It: Focus on one task at a time for better efficiency.*
2. Start Your Day with the "Frog":
   - *Tackle your hardest task first thing in the morning to feel accomplished and lighten your mental load.*

3. The Gratitude Reset:
   - *Write down three things you're grateful for every day — it shifts focus from stress to abundance.*

Moments to Ground You

- Sip your coffee in silence before the day begins.
- Let the sunlight warm your face during a quiet walk.
- Write one kind word to yourself at the end of each day.

Reclaiming Joy

- Pick up that book you've been meaning to read.
- Dance like no one's watching — even if the kids are!
- Spend five minutes sketching, journaling, or simply breathing.

These are not distractions; they are declarations. "I deserve this."

Let Children Join the Journey

Caring for yourself teaches children that self-care is strength, not selfishness.

Involve Them

- Cooking Together: Let them stir, chop (safely), or set the table.
- Gardening Together: Share the joy of nurturing plants or creating a small herb garden.
- Movement Together: Stretch, dance, or do yoga poses side by side.

Show Them Joy

- Let them see you laugh freely, rest unapologetically, and pursue your passions.
- Celebrate small joys with them — whether it's spotting a rainbow or sharing a funny story.

In loving yourself, you teach them how to love themselves too.

The Guilt Detox: Breaking Free from Self-Criticism

Taking time for yourself often comes with a side of guilt. Here's how to let go:

1. Reframe Guilt:
    - *Instead of thinking, "I shouldn't need time for myself," say, "Caring for myself helps me care for my family better."*
2. Celebrate Progress:
    - *Acknowledge the small wins: "I took a five-minute walk today, and it felt great."*
3. Say This Affirmation:
    - *"I matter. My well-being is essential."*
4. Replace Perfection with Presence:
    - *Remember, children do not need a perfect parent. They need a present one.*

THE SECOND SECRET: CARE

Self-Care Toolkit: Quick Tips and Strategies

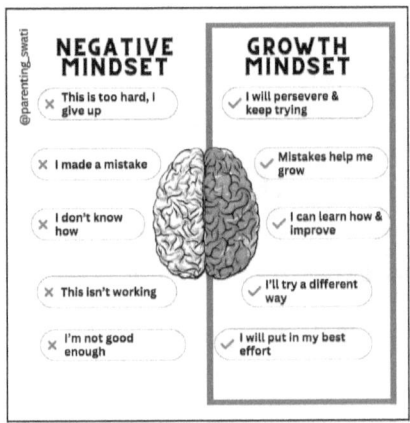

Figure 28

Physical Care
- Gentle stretching in the morning or before bed.
- Take a quick walk, even if it's around the house.
- Hydrate! A glass of water can be a mini refresh.

Mental and Emotional Care
- Box Breathing: Inhale for 4 counts, hold for 4, exhale for 4, and hold for 4.
- Emotion Jars: Write down small joys or affirmations, and pull one out when you need a boost.
- Mindfulness Minute: Spend 60 seconds focusing on your breath or observing your surroundings.

Social Self-Care

- Connect with other parents in playgroups or online communities.

THE SECOND SECRET: CARE

- Schedule a coffee date with a friend — even if it's virtual.
- Don't hesitate to ask for help — parenting is a team effort!

The Bigger Picture: Self-Care Is Love in Action

Parenthood is a dance of giving and receiving. As you pour love into children's world, don't forget to refill your own cup.

- Celebrate Your Humanity: You don't have to be perfect. Being present, even imperfectly, is more than enough.
- Cherish the Moments: Parenting isn't about getting it all done — it's about embracing the beautiful chaos with grace.

Gratitude Journal Activity

1. Set a Time: Choose a time each day (e.g., morning or before bed) to write in your journal.
2. Write 3 Things: List three things you are grateful for that day. They can be big or small!
3. Reflect: Write a few words about why you are grateful for each item.
4. Review Weekly: At the end of the week, look back at your entries to see how your gratitude has grown.

A simple, daily practice to focus on positivity and boost your mood! ✨

A Love Letter to You, the Parent

Dear Parent,

Your journey is nothing short of extraordinary. Amid the challenges and love, you give endlessly — your time, energy, and heart. But here's a gentle reminder: you can't pour from an empty cup.

THE SECOND SECRET: CARE

Prioritize your well-being, not out of selfishness, but because your family thrives when *you* thrive.

Children don't need a perfect parent — they need *you*: vibrant, joyful, and rested.

Take the walk. Dance in the kitchen. Celebrate the little wins. You're doing an incredible job, and your family is so lucky to have you. 🌟

Self-Care: Your Super-Parent Fuel

Self-care isn't selfish — it's the fuel that powers your parenting superpowers. Some days you'll soar, other days you'll simply get by, and that's okay. What matters is showing up — with love for children and kindness toward yourself.

So ,sip your coffee, take that breather, or enjoy a chocolate bar in peace. You're doing amazing, and the care you show yourself today shapes a brighter tomorrow for you and your family. 💗

There are few other things which are a part of self- care
1. Why decluttering is a game changer for both parents and children?
2. What is a blue print of growth and connection?
3. How can the father child bond be inseparable?

Mom & Dad, remember! You are husband-wife first and then parents.

3.1 Why Decluttering Is Game Changer?

Parenting is a beautiful yet demanding journey that often leaves you feeling like you're juggling a thousand things at once. The

3.1 WHY DECLUTTERING IS GAME CHANGER?

chaos of everyday life — be it physical clutter at home or mental clutter from endless notifications — can add unnecessary stress, making it harder to focus on what truly matters: your family. This is where decluttering becomes a game changer, not just for your personal well-being but for your role as a parent.

Decluttering is the process of removing unnecessary items, distractions, or commitments from your life to create space for clarity, peace, and joy. It's not just about tidying up — it's about simplifying your environment and your mind so you can prioritize what truly matters.

Decluttering can take many forms:

1. Physical Decluttering: Simplifying your home by removing excess items that no longer serve you.
2. Digital Decluttering: Organizing your digital space to reduce distractions and stress.
3. Time Decluttering: Streamlining your calendar to leave room for meaningful moments.
4. Mental Decluttering: Letting go of thoughts or commitments that weigh you down.

Parenting requires focus, patience, and emotional availability — qualities that are hard to nurture in a chaotic environment. Here's how decluttering supports your parenting journey:

1. Reduces Stress:
    - *A tidy home and organized digital life translate to a calmer mind. When you're less stressed, you're more present for children.*

THE SECOND SECRET: CARE

2. Teaches Valuable Lessons:
   - *By involving children in the decluttering process, you instill important values like minimalism, gratitude, and organization.*
3. Fosters Quality Time:
   - *Simplifying your environment and schedule creates space for joyful, distraction-free moments with your family.*
4. Encourages Emotional Clarity:
   - *Letting go of unnecessary commitments and toxic influences allows you to focus on what truly matters, helping you respond to children with patience and understanding.*
5. Boosts Productivity:
   - *An organized environment means less time spent searching for things or managing clutter, leaving you more time to engage with your family.*

Decluttering Hacks for a Happier Life

Digital Decluttering

- **Delete Stressful Apps:** If an app doesn't add value or joy, uninstall it.
- **Unfollow Negativity:** Say goodbye to toxic social media accounts.
- **Mute Notifications:** Silence distractions during family time to stay present.
- **Organize Your Phone:** Clear out unnecessary files, sort your gallery, and clean your inbox.
- **Set Boundaries:** Use "Do Not Disturb" or app timers to focus on family moments.

Pro Tip: A tidy phone = a tidy mind.

3.1 WHY DECLUTTERING IS GAME CHANGER?

Home Decluttering

- Start Small: Begin with a single drawer or shelf. Small victories build momentum.
- Toys on Rotation: Donate or store toys that haven't been used in six months.
- 1 In, 1 Out: For every new item brought home, remove one old item.
- Clothes Cleanout: If you haven't worn it in a year, donate it.

Pro Tip: Less stuff = more joy.

Family-Friendly Decluttering

- Clutter Basket: Use a basket to gather stray items daily and empty it regularly.
- Declutter Race: Make tidying up fun by setting a timer and turning it into a game.
- Memory Box: Keep the best of your kids' artwork and take photos of the rest.

Pro Tip: Turn tidying up into a family bonding activity.

Simplify Your Calendar

- Say "No": Learn to skip non-essential commitments to avoid burnout.
- Leave Room for Fun: Empty spaces in your schedule allow for spontaneous joy.

Pro Tip: A simple schedule = a happy schedule.

A clutter-free life means less stress and more smiles. It's about finding freedom in simplicity so you can show up as your best self for your family. Start small, stay consistent, and watch as the peace of a decluttered life transforms your parenting experience. 🎉

By decluttering your space, your time, and your mind, you not only create a more harmonious environment but also set a powerful example for children about the value of simplicity and intentionality. It's not just tidying — it's creating space for a happier, more connected family life.

3.2 A Blueprint for Growth and Connection

Parenting is like juggling — the balls are your toddler's tantrums, your preteen's questions, and your teen's quest for independence. It's not about having all the answers; it's about showing up with love, consistency, and the tools to guide children through life's ups and downs. This chapter combines conflict resolution, navigating transitions, and practical tools into a roadmap for raising resilient, confident, and emotionally intelligent kids — without losing your mind (or your coffee).

Conflict Resolution: Turning Chaos into Connection

Whether it's over screen time, curfews, or who gets the last cookie, disagreements are inevitable. But here's the secret: conflict isn't failure; it's a chance to teach life skills like empathy, problem-solving, and boundary-setting.

Why Conflict Happens at Different Ages

1. Toddlers: Testing limits and asserting autonomy. E.g.- Meltdowns because they want the blue cup (not the red one!).

3.2 A BLUEPRINT FOR GROWTH AND CONNECTION

2. School-Aged Kids: Navigating rules, fairness, and responsibilities. E.g.- Disagreements over chores or sharing toys.
3. Teenagers: Seeking independence and challenging authority. E.g.- Debates over curfews or screen time limits.

Age-Appropriate Strategies

- Toddlers: Redirect and stay calm. "You can't play with the plug, but let's build a tower with these blocks."
- School-Aged Kids: Involve them in solutions. "What's a fair way to split your screen time with your sibling?"
- Preteens and Teenagers: Listen, validate, and collaborate on boundaries. "I understand why you feel the curfew is strict. Let's find a compromise that works for both of us."

Setting Boundaries: The Love in "No"

Boundaries aren't about control — they're about safety, respect, and mutual understanding. Clear, consistent rules give kids the structure they need to thrive while teaching them accountability and respect for others.

The "Two Choices" Rule

Avoid power struggles by offering limited options:
- *Example*: "Do you want to brush your teeth before or after putting on your pajamas?"

Repair Relationships After Conflict

Mistakes happen — on both sides. Apologizing models accountability.

- *Example*: "I'm sorry I lost my temper earlier. Let's talk about how we can handle this better next time."

Navigating Transitions: Guiding Through Change

Whether it's starting school, moving houses, or adjusting to a new sibling, life transitions can feel like emotional earthquakes for kids. Your steady guidance helps them adapt and thrive.

Strategies for Smooth Transitions

1. Prepare in Advance: "We're visiting your new school tomorrow to meet your teacher and see your classroom."
2. Involve Them: "How would you like to decorate your new room?"
3. Acknowledge Their Feelings: "It's okay to feel nervous about moving. I feel that way too sometimes."

Building Resilience Through Transitions

- Celebrate small wins: "You were so brave meeting your new classmates today!"
- Model adaptability: "Starting a new job is a bit scary for me too, but I know we'll adjust together."

Practical Tools for Everyday Parenting

Let's face it — parenting is unpredictable. Having a toolbox of strategies can make all the difference.

The Golden Hour Bonding Strategy

The hour before bedtime is a magical window for connection and emotional security.

3.2 A BLUEPRINT FOR GROWTH AND CONNECTION

- Toddlers: Storytelling with values. "Let's read about a bunny who learns to share."
- School-Aged Kids: Reflect on the day. "What made you smile today?"
- Teenagers: Foster open dialogue. "Anything on your mind before bed?"

Cheat Sheet for Common Challenges

1. Tantrums: Redirect attention and name emotions. *Example*: "You're upset because you can't have candy right now. Let's play with your puzzle instead."
2. Defiance: Collaborate rather than command. *Example*: "I understand you don't want to do your homework now. When do you think would be a good time?"
3. Independence: Gradually give more responsibility. *Example*: "Can you organize your school supplies this week?"

Unique Tools to Try

1. Emotion Jars: Fill a jar with calming activities (e.g., "Draw a picture" or "Take five deep breaths"). Use it during emotional storms.
2. The YES-NO-AND Technique: Redirect behavior while validating feelings. *Example*: "Yes, I see you're excited to play outside, and it's time for dinner. We can play afterward."
3. Family Agreements: Create a shared "contract" for values and rules. *Example*: "We agree to have a screen-free dinner every night."

THE SECOND SECRET: CARE

The Bigger Picture: Parenting with Intention and Empathy

Parenting isn't about avoiding conflict or challenges — it's about navigating them with love, consistency, and humor. Every tantrum, negotiation, or life transition is a chance to teach resilience, foster independence, and deepen your connection with children.

Remember:

- Conflict is a teaching moment: It's an opportunity to model respect and empathy.
- Boundaries show love: They teach safety and self-respect.
- Transitions build resilience: Change is part of life, and guiding children through it equips them for the future.

You've got this. Whether it's managing a meltdown, celebrating a win, or simply getting through another day, every moment you invest in children strengthens the foundation of a confident, compassionate adult.

Take a deep breath, grab your "parenting toolbox," and trust the process. Together, you and children are navigating this beautiful, messy, transformative journey — one laugh, hug, and "teachable moment" at a time.

Looking Ahead to Lifelong Connection

As your children grow, your relationship evolves. The toddler who clung to you, the child who asked endless questions, and the teenager asserting their independence — all are stages in a lifelong bond that deepens over time.

- Your Role Will Change: You'll move from being a manager to a mentor, and eventually, to a trusted confidant. The values,

love, and lessons you've instilled will guide children even when they are navigating life on their own.
- **Their Independence Is Your Success:** Watching them soar might bring bittersweet moments, but it's the ultimate testament to your efforts.

A Message to You, the Incredible Parent

Parenthood isn't always easy, but you've shown up with courage, creativity, and an unshakable commitment to children's well-being.

- **You Are Enough:** In every messy, chaotic, and beautiful moment, you've been the parent your child needs.
- **Your Journey Is Profound:** Through tantrums, triumphs, late-night worries, and early-morning cuddles, you've built a legacy of love and resilience.

Parting Thoughts

As you continue this journey, remember that parenting isn't about rigid rules or perfect decisions. It's about connection, adaptation, and love.

- **Lean Into the Joys:** Savor the laughter, the hugs, and the tiny, fleeting moments that remind you why this journey is worth it.
- **Embrace the Challenges:** Each challenge is an opportunity to teach, grow, and deepen your bond with children.
- **Celebrate the Path Ahead:** Parenting doesn't end; it transforms. Your bond with children is a lifelong treasure, a foundation that will carry both of you through all of life's seasons.

THE SECOND SECRET: CARE

To You and Your Family

To the parent who keeps showing up, even on the hard days.

To the child who flourishes because of your love and guidance.

To the future, bright with endless possibilities.

Thank you for walking this journey of love, learning, and connection.

Here's to the memories you've created, the lessons you've learned, and the remarkable story you're still writing — together.

With love and gratitude,

Here's to you and the lifelong bond you share. ♡

3.3 The Father-Child Bond: Building Connection Through Presence and Respect

Fatherhood is a powerful journey of influence, love, and purpose. While children often form natural attachments to their mothers, fathers have a distinct and transformative role in their child's emotional and social development. Through small, consistent acts of care, respect, and connection, fathers can create bonds that are as deep and enduring as they are meaningful. Fathers role is just not providers they are nurtures too. I have seen it in my house too when I see my husband getting them ready. I feel so proud of my husband, because he is a true gentleman.

Even the word "gentleman" starts with "gentle."

Boys don't need to be macho or tough all the time — they need to learn that real strength comes from kindness and compassion.

When fathers show gentleness — through patience, respect, and care — they teach their sons emotional values that stay for life. Boys who see this grow up knowing that being gentle doesn't make you weak; it makes you a true gentleman.

According to a Harvard study, a <u>father's mindset is directly proportional to their child's mindset</u>. Children often take their cues from their father's behavior and outlook, mirroring their actions and values. For example, if a father prioritizes fitness and leads an active lifestyle, the child is likely to adopt a similar mindset about health and fitness. Kids literally take the blueprint from the father.

The same principle applies to respect and relationships. If a father shows genuine respect and care for the women in his life, the child will internalize this behavior and carry it into their own relationships. A father's actions and mindset create a blueprint that profoundly influences how a child views and navigates the world. By leading with positive values, fathers set a foundation for their children to thrive.

The Role of Fathers: Presence, Purpose, and Respect

Fathers shape their child's sense of self, their emotional resilience, and their understanding of relationships.

Why Fathers Matter

1. Emotional Anchor: Fathers provide stability and reassurance, helping children navigate life's complexities with confidence.
2. Role Models for Growth: Children learn kindness, respect, and resilience by observing their father's actions.

THE SECOND SECRET: CARE

3. Respect Starts at Home: When fathers show love and respect for their child's mother, they model healthy relationships.

Key Insight: Children notice how you treat their mother. Respect builds admiration, trust, and love in your bond with them.

Emotional Perspective

Your presence matters more than perfection. The love, care, and time you invest create a safe and nurturing space for children's growth. Show them your leader side and achiever side of yours so that kids see the father as a strong and balanced personality.

Building and Strengthening the Father-Child Bond

Fathers don't need grand gestures; small, consistent acts of love and attention have the greatest impact.

1. The Power of Presence: Be present in their lives, from cheering at soccer games to bedtime stories. Dedicate regular "Dad Time" for uninterrupted activities your children enjoy. Your availability shows that they are valued and loved.
2. Active Listening: Focus fully on children's words, validating their thoughts and emotions.
   - Example Prompt:
     o *"What's something that made you laugh today?"*
3. Bond Through Shared Activities: Tailor bonding moments to their interests and developmental stage:
   o *Toddlers: Build pillow forts or play hide-and-seek.*
   o *School-Aged Kids: Solve puzzles, play sports, or bake together.*
   o *Teens: Work on hobbies, cook meals, or have open conversations during car rides.*

3.3 THE FATHER-CHILD BOND

Fathers as Emotional Role Models

Emotional intelligence begins at home. Fathers can teach emotional regulation and vulnerability by leading through example.

1. Show, Don't Just Tell: Share your emotions and coping strategies openly. Example: "I felt frustrated earlier, so I took a walk to clear my head. What helps you when you're upset?" It's okay to cry and share emotions, gone were the days "BOYS DON'T CRY". Boys do cry and it's good to vent out emotions.
2. Practice Co-Regulation with Younger Children: Stay calm during children's meltdowns to help them navigate big emotions. Practice calming techniques like deep breathing together.
3. Create a Safe Space for Emotional Sharing: When children feel safe expressing their feelings, they develop emotional resilience.
    - Conversation Starter: "You seem a little down today — do you want to talk about it?"

Respecting the Mother: The Core of Healthy Modeling

Your relationship with the child's mother profoundly impacts how they view love, respect, and partnership.

1. Be a Role Model: Use kind words, practice patience, and support her decisions, especially in front of your children. Example: "Your mom worked really hard to make this day special for us. Let's say thank you together."
    - This truly matters as the children see their father as a benchmark for relationships. Respect toward their mother fosters admiration and builds trust in your bond with them.

THE SECOND SECRET: CARE

Fostering Independence and Resilience

A father's guidance in problem-solving and perseverance helps children navigate challenges with confidence.

1. Encourage Problem-Solving: Guide, don't solve. Example "What do you think is the best way to fix this? Let's figure it out together."
2. Celebrate Effort Over Results: Focusing on effort builds a growth mindset and resilience.
    - *Affirmation Example: "I'm proud of how you kept trying even when it was hard."*

Navigating Challenges in Fatherhood

Parenting comes with its hurdles, but small, intentional changes make a big difference.

1. Balancing Work and Family: Create family rituals like tech-free dinners or weekly outings.
2. Overcoming Emotional Barriers: Start Small: Express love consistently with affirmations like:
    - "I love spending time with you."
    - "I'm proud of you."

Bonding Through Life Stages

As children grow, their needs evolve, but your consistent love and presence remain key.

1. Toddlers and Preschoolers (0–5 Years)- Bedtime stories or "chase-and-giggle" games.
2. School-Aged Children (6–12 Years)- Crafting, outdoor adventures, or working on projects together.

3. Teenagers (13–18 Years)- Deep conversations during shared activities, like driving or cooking.

A Father's Legacy

The everyday acts of love and care create a lasting impact on children's sense of self and their future relationships.

Reflection Prompt:

"What memory do I want my child to carry with them? How can I create more moments like that?"

A Final Word to Fathers

Dear Dad,

Your role is pivotal, and children see you as their guide, their hero, and their safe space. Every time you listen, respect, and show love, you're shaping their world for the better.

When you honor their mother, you teach them the essence of respect and partnership. When you show up — whether through play, conversation, or a simple hug — you're saying, "You matter to me."

You don't need to be perfect; you just need to be present. In the little moments of connection, you're creating a legacy of love that will resonate through generations.

Keep showing up, dad. You're their greatest example of strength, kindness, and love — and you're doing an incredible job. ✺

3.4 Strengthening the Husband-Wife Relationship

Parenting often takes center stage in family life, but maintaining a strong bond with your partner is equally important. A healthy, loving relationship between spouses not only benefits you as individuals but also creates a stable and nurturing environment for children. Here, we'll explore the importance of intimacy and strategies to strengthen your bond as partners.

Why the Husband-Wife Bond Matters

Foundation of the Family: A strong partnership provides emotional security for children and sets an example of love, respect, and teamwork.

Emotional Resilience: A connected relationship helps you navigate the challenges of parenting together.

Happiness Overflow: When you prioritize your relationship, the happiness you share overflows into the entire family dynamic.

Common Challenges

Time Constraints: Between work, parenting, and household responsibilities, finding time for each other can be tough.

Emotional Exhaustion: The demands of parenting often leave little energy for intimacy.

Communication Gaps: Stress can lead to misunderstandings or reduced meaningful conversations.

Evolving Roles: Shifting from a romantic partnership to co-parents can change dynamics.

3.4 STRENGTHENING THE HUSBAND-WIFE RELATIONSHIP

Strategies to Strengthen Your Bond

1. Make Time for Each Other- Quality time helps you reconnect and reminds you why you fell in love in the first place.
   - Date Nights: Schedule regular date nights, even if it's just a quiet dinner at home after the kids are asleep.
   - Micro-Moments: Share small moments daily — morning coffee together, a quick hug before work, or a shared laugh over something trivial.
   - Plan Mini-Getaways: Even a day trip can refresh your connection and give you uninterrupted time together.

2. Communicate Openly- Honest, empathetic communication is the cornerstone of any strong relationship.
   - Daily Check-Ins: Spend 10–15 minutes daily talking about your day without distractions. Focus on emotions, not logistics.
   - Express Gratitude: Say "thank you" often — for small gestures or simply for being there.
   - Discuss Challenges: Address issues calmly before they escalate. Use "I" statements (e.g., "I feel overwhelmed when...") instead of blaming.

3. Reignite Intimacy- Physical and emotional intimacy deepens your connection and builds trust.
   - Prioritize Physical Touch: Small gestures like holding hands, hugs, or a kiss goodbye can rekindle closeness.
   - Create a Romantic Atmosphere: Surprise your partner with a candlelit dinner, a heartfelt note, or a playlist of your favorite songs.

THE SECOND SECRET: CARE

- Talk About Intimacy Needs: Be open about what you both need to feel connected. Remove guilt or shame from the conversation.

4. Share Responsibilities- Sharing parenting and household duties reduces stress and builds teamwork.
   - Divide and Conquer: Clearly split responsibilities to avoid one partner feeling overwhelmed.
   - Switch Roles Occasionally: Try swapping tasks to appreciate each other's efforts.
   - Tag Team Breaks: Alternate "me-time" moments, so you both get opportunities to recharge.

5. Support Each Other's Goals- Encouraging individual growth strengthens mutual respect and admiration.
   - Celebrate Achievements: Acknowledge each other's successes, whether big or small.
   - Pursue Hobbies Together: Find shared interests, such as cooking, gardening, or taking a class.
   - Respect Individual Time: Support each other's personal goals and the time needed to pursue them.

6. Laugh Together- Humor can dissolve tension and bring you closer.
   - Inside Jokes: Keep alive the silly things that make you both laugh.
   - Light-Hearted Conversations: Talk about fun topics, avoiding heavy or stressful subjects during relaxed times.
   - Watch Comedy Together: Enjoy movies or shows that make you both laugh and let you unwind.

3.4 STRENGTHENING THE HUSBAND-WIFE RELATIONSHIP

7. Seek Help When Needed- a neutral perspective can provide clarity and solutions.
   - Counseling or Therapy: Consider couples counseling to work through challenges or strengthen your relationship.
   - Parenting Support Groups: You can join www.joyfulparenting.club for a close networking community.

Practical Tips for Busy Parents

- Nightly Connection Ritual: Spend 5 minutes expressing what you appreciated about each other that day.
- Love Notes: Leave small notes of affection in unexpected places, like a wallet, bag, or pillow.
- Technology-Free Zone: Dedicate one evening a week to unplugging from devices and focusing solely on each other.
- Create a "Couples Bucket List": Plan future activities or trips that excite both of you, fostering a sense of shared purpose.

PRO TIP: *The 2:2:2 Family Rule*

1. Every 2 Weeks: Go on a date night with your partner — keep the spark alive!
2. Every 2 Months: Plan a family outing or day trip — bond over fun adventures.
3. Every 2 Years: Take a family vacation — create memories to last a lifetime.

This Strengthens relationships, breaks routines, and brings everyone closer. Simple, intentional, and effective! ♡

Think about your family's traditions. How can you incorporate them into this strategy?

THE SECOND SECRET: CARE

Parenting is an odyssey — a journey that transforms not only children but also you. It's a path full of surprises, challenges, and immeasurable joys. As we wrap up this shared adventure, let's pause to reflect on the love, growth, and resilience that have defined your journey as a parent.

The Bigger Picture

A strong husband-wife relationship doesn't happen by chance — it requires intentional effort, communication, and love. By prioritizing your connection, you not only enrich your partnership but also create a happy, harmonious environment for your family. Remember, nurturing your bond as a couple is one of the best gifts you can give children — a home filled with love and mutual respect.

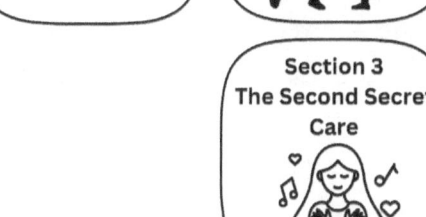

Your Parenting Journey

SECTION 4

THE THIRD SECRET : CELEBRATE

Family Bliss & Beauty of Diverse Parenting

𝒫arenting is like cooking — every family has its own unique recipe. Some include the spice of joint families, others savor the simplicity of single parenting, and a few stir in the zest of co-parenting or the sweetness of grandparents. The beauty is that there's no one "right" way to create a family full of love, connection, and a sprinkle of chaos.

Whether you're managing a bustling household, navigating co-parenting post-divorce, or relying on the wisdom of grandparents, family bliss isn't about perfection — it's about connection. It's in the shared laughs, traditions, and those magical moments where you pause and think, "We're doing alright."

So, let's dive into the heart of modern family life, where boundaries are set with love, traditions bind us together, and every parenting style gets its moment to shine. Because no matter the setup, family is where love grows — and that's always worth celebrating. 💖

Let's dive into:

4.1 How to celebrate parenthood as a Single Parent
4.2 How can Divorced Parent be the best version of themselves and celebrate parenting?
4.3 How is the mission possible to manage Sibling Rivalry?
4.4 How can kids celebrate Joint Family and Grand Parents?

4.1 Thriving as a Single Parent : Parenting Isn't One Size Fits All

Parenting solo is a journey of resilience, creativity, and deep love. It's about balancing the day-to-day chaos with the immense responsibility of shaping a child's world, often while managing life's challenges with fewer hands-on deck. But while single parenting can feel overwhelming at times, it's also an opportunity to build a unique and profound bond with children.

This chapter celebrates the strength of single parents while offering practical strategies and heartfelt encouragement to navigate the road with confidence and grace.

You're Not Alone: Building Your Village

Single parenting doesn't mean doing it all on your own. Building a strong support network can lighten the load and bring joy to the journey.

Practical Tips:

- Embrace Your Tribe: Reach out to family, friends, neighbors, or local parenting groups. Babysitting swaps, carpooling

arrangements, or even a shared meal plan can make a huge difference.
- Create a "Go-To" Circle: Write down three people you can call for emotional or practical support during tough moments.

Perspective Shift:

Asking for help isn't a sign of weakness; it's a reminder that parenting is a collective effort. Let children see the beauty of community and connection in action.

Also, I have added a section on nannies in the foundational age Section 2.1.1. Refer to it for a better understanding.

The Power of Small Self-Care Moments

Caring for yourself may feel like a luxury, but it's a necessity. Taking even small steps to recharge can improve your well-being and set a powerful example for children.

Quick Self-Care Ideas:
- Micro Moments of Joy: Enjoy a cup of tea, take five deep breaths, or listen to your favorite playlist during errands.
- Anchor Rituals: Create daily routines, like lighting a candle at dinner or journaling one thought of gratitude.

Why It Matters:

By showing children that self-care is important, you teach them the value of self-respect and emotional health. A rested and happy parent is better equipped to tackle the challenges of parenting.

4.1 THRIVING AS A SINGLE PARENT

Reframing the "Do-It-All" Myth

The world may celebrate single parents as superheroes who "do it all," but perfection isn't the goal — it's connection. Focus on what matters most: a loving, secure relationship with children.

Strategies for Balance:

- Celebrate Small Wins: Whether it's getting through bedtime or completing a school project, celebrate every victory — big or small.
- Lean Into Your Strengths: Whether it's humor, creativity, or patience, recognize and use what makes you a great parent.
- Embrace Imperfection: No one gets everything right, and that's okay. Children value your love far more than your ability to check off a to-do list.

Perspective Shift:

You're not here to "do it all." You're here to love, guide, and show up for children — and that's more than enough.

A Personal Note to You

Dear Single Parent,

You're walking a unique path filled with challenges, triumphs, and unforgettable moments.

- It's Okay to Feel Tired: Parenting is hard work, and you're human.
- It's Okay to Lean on Others: Asking for help isn't a weakness — it's a testament to your strength.

- It's Okay to Prioritize Yourself: A little time for self-care goes a long way for you and your children.

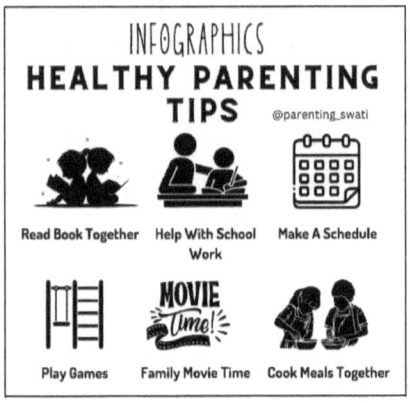

Figure 29

In the late nights, the endless questions, and the unexpected joys, you're creating something extraordinary: a bond built on unconditional love and unwavering resilience. Here's to your strength, your love, and the beautiful story you're writing together. You've got this. 💖

4.2 Co-Parenting After Divorce: Building Stability and Harmony for Children

Co-parenting after divorce is like walking a tightrope, with children's happiness and stability as the balancing pole. While this journey may come with emotional complexities, it offers a unique opportunity to model resilience, respect, and unconditional love.

Let's explore how to navigate this dynamic with practical strategies and an unwavering focus on children's well-being.

4.2 CO-PARENTING AFTER DIVORCE

The Foundation: Open Communication

Clear, respectful communication is the backbone of successful co-parenting. While past emotions may linger, keeping conversations focused on children fosters a constructive relationship.

Practical Strategies:

- Set Clear Boundaries: Use co-parenting apps like Our Family Wizard or Talking Parents to streamline schedules and share updates without miscommunication.
- Regular Updates: Keep each other informed about school progress, extracurriculars, and health matters via email or messages.
- Neutral Language: Treat co-parenting like a professional partnership, keeping discussions respectful and child-centered.

Emotional Perspective:

You don't have to agree on every detail, but when communication is calm and consistent, children feel reassured by a united front.

Consistency Across Two Homes

Children thrive on predictability. Maintaining consistent routines and rules between homes creates a sense of stability and security.

Practical Strategies:

- Align on Core Rules: Agree on basics like bedtime, screen time, and discipline to minimize confusion.
- Shared Calendar: Use a digital calendar to manage visitation schedules, school events, and activities.

- Comfort Items: Let children bring familiar items — like a favorite stuffed animal or backpack — between homes for added comfort.

Emotional Perspective:

Consistency sends a powerful message: No matter where children are their world is steady, loving, and secure.

Shifting the Focus: It's About the Child

Successful co-parenting isn't about revisiting the past; it's about building a future where children feel supported and cherished.

Practical Strategies:

- Avoid Criticism: Speak positively or neutrally about the other parent, especially in front of children, to protect their sense of safety and loyalty.
- Celebrate Together: Attend milestones like birthdays or graduations as a united presence whenever possible.
- Support Relationships: Encourage children's bond with the other parent, even if it's emotionally challenging for you.

Emotional Perspective:

Children's love isn't divided between homes — it's expanded. Fostering a collaborative dynamic creates an environment where they can flourish without feeling torn.

Handling Conflict with Grace

Disagreements are inevitable, but how you handle them shapes the co-parenting experience for children.

Unique Approaches:
- Parallel Parenting: If communication is challenging, limit interaction by managing separate responsibilities while sharing key updates.
- Child-First Filter: Before reacting, pause and ask yourself, "How will this affect my child?" Let their needs guide your response.
- Conflict Resolution Steps:
  - *Pause: Take a moment to cool down.*
  - *Plan: Reflect on the issue and potential solutions.*
  - *Propose: Present your ideas with clarity and respect, always keeping the focus on children.*

A Personal Note to Co-Parents

Dear Co-parent,

Co-parenting after divorce is a testament to your love and commitment to children. It's not always easy, but every step you take to prioritize their happiness and stability is a gift they'll carry for life.

- Celebrate Progress: Co-parenting is about making consistent efforts, not achieving flawless harmony.
- Model Collaboration: Even small acts of teamwork show children the power of respect and unity.
- Practice Self-Compassion: Extend grace to yourself and your co-parent — this journey is as much about growth as it is about love.

Children will remember the care and effort you poured into creating a stable, loving world for them. Together, you're teaching them resilience, respect, and the enduring strength of family, even when it spans two homes.

You've got this — and the love you share with children will always light the way forward. 💗

4.3 Managing Sibling Rivalry with Love and Understanding

Sibling rivalry — those squabbles, shouts, and stolen toys — can feel exhausting, but beneath the surface lies an opportunity to build bonds that last a lifetime. It's natural for siblings to clash as they navigate their relationships, but with a little patience, empathy, and love, these moments can become powerful lessons in connection, teamwork, and understanding.

This chapter is about helping you turn those moments of conflict into stepping stones for deeper sibling love, no matter their age.

Why Do Siblings Rival?

Imagine this: your older child was the center of your world, basking in undivided attention. Then one day, a tiny newcomer arrives, demanding their place. It's no wonder they feel displaced. Or maybe, as they grow, they compete to feel special or validated, looking to you for fairness and love.

The good news? Rivalry isn't a sign of failure — it's a sign of growth. It means they're learning to navigate relationships, share resources, and express emotions. And with your guidance, they can transform those struggles into lifelong skills.

4.3 MANAGING SIBLING RIVALRY

1 to 5 Years: The Little Explorers

At this stage, everything feels like a battle for your attention. Toddlers and preschoolers are just beginning to understand sharing and fairness, and it can be tough for them to wait their turn or see someone else get the spotlight.

Challenges:
- "That's mine!" arguments over toys.
- Jealousy over time spent with a sibling.
- Big emotions in little bodies — tantrums, tears, and more.

How to Guide Them with Love:

1. Show Them They're Special: Spend one-on-one moments with each child, even if it's just reading their favorite book before bed. Let them know their place in your heart is secure.
2. Teach Sharing Through Play: Make sharing fun with games like passing balls back and forth or building towers together.
3. Be Their Referee, Not Their Judge: Instead of saying, "Why can't you be like your sister?" try, "I see you both want the toy — how can we take turns?"
4. Praise Cooperation: When they work together, celebrate it. "I love how you both built that tower — it looks amazing!"

Heartfelt Tip: When children struggle to share, try kneeling down and saying, "I know it's hard to let go of your favorite toy. You're doing such a great job learning to share."

6 to 12 Years: The Growing Bonds

By now, children are more independent, and their worlds are expanding. But with independence comes comparison — who's better at school, sports, or chores? Rivalry here often stems from wanting to feel equally loved and seen.

Challenges:
- Feeling like rules or attention aren't fair.
- Arguments about personal space or belongings.
- Competing for praise and recognition.

How to Guide Them with Love:

1. Celebrate Their Individuality: Remind them they're not competing — they're unique. Say, "I love how creative you are with art, and I admire how kind your sibling is to friends."
2. Turn Competition into Teamwork: Assign collaborative tasks like baking cookies or tidying the living room together. Reward their teamwork with praise or a family treat.
3. Teach Problem-Solving: When they argue, don't jump in to solve it. Instead, guide them with, "How can you work together to make this fair?"
4. Spend Quality Time: Set aside "special time" for each child — whether it's playing catch, baking, or just talking. This reassures them they don't need to compete for your love.

Heartfelt Tip: Use phrases like, "I love you both for who you are, not what you do. You don't need to be the same — you're both amazing in your own way."

13 to 19 Years: The Journey to Adulthood

The teenage years are a time of identity and independence. Siblings may clash over privileges, privacy, or personality differences. But it's also a time when they can form stronger bonds — if nurtured carefully.

Challenges:

- Privacy and personal space disputes.
- Resentment over differences in rules or freedoms.
- Feeling overshadowed or misunderstood.

How to Guide Them with Love:

1. Respect Their Boundaries: Give them space when they need it and set clear rules about respecting each other's belongings.
2. Encourage Open Communication: When conflicts arise, let them express their feelings without fear of judgment. Say, "Tell me what's bothering you so we can figure this out together."
3. Explain Fairness, Not Equality: If rules differ because of age, explain why. "Your older sibling has a later curfew because they're older and more experienced."
4. Foster Shared Interests: Help them find common ground, like a shared hobby, family tradition, or project. Even watching a favorite movie together can create bonds.

Heartfelt Tip: Remind them, "You don't have to be best friends, but you'll always have each other. Take care of one another."

Universal Strategies for All Ages

Some strategies transcend age, working to foster harmony at every stage:

- Stay Neutral: Avoid playing favorites. Focus on solving the issue, not blaming.
- Model Respect: Let them see you handle disagreements calmly and respectfully.
- Promote Empathy: Ask questions like, "How do you think your sibling felt when that happened?"

- Create Moments of Connection: Hold family game nights, cook meals together, or start traditions that bring everyone closer.

Activities to Strengthen Bonds

1. Sibling Jar: Write down fun activities (like building forts or making pancakes) and pick one when tensions rise.
2. Turn-Taking Cards: Create a system for sharing high-demand items, like favorite games or devices.
3. Kindness Chart: Track acts of kindness between siblings, rewarding them for cooperation and care.

The Bigger Picture

Sibling rivalry isn't about eliminating conflict — it's about teaching love, respect, and teamwork. Through each squabble and hug, children are learning how to navigate relationships, handle emotions, and value one another.

When the noise of bickering fades, the love they build will echo for a lifetime. As a parent, you're the steady hand guiding them, the heart connecting them, and the gentle voice reminding them, "You'll always have each other." Keep going — you're creating something beautiful.

4.4 Grandparents and Joint Families – Bridging Generations, Building Bonds

Life in a multigenerational family is like a symphony — filled with harmonious notes, a few clashing chords, and an undeniable rhythm of love and connection. Whether grandparents are stepping into caregiving roles or you're raising children in a joint family,

4.4 GRAND PARENTS AND JOINT FAMILIES

this chapter celebrates the beauty, challenges, and life lessons of living across generations.

Grandparents as Caregivers: Tradition Meets Modernity

Stepping into the caregiver role as a grandparent is a profound gift. It's an opportunity to pass down family traditions while adapting to the evolving needs of a new generation.

The Unique Bond: Love Rooted in Legacy

Grandparents provide more than daily care; they offer a sense of history, identity, and unconditional love.

- Emotional Perspective: Your shared moments — bedtime stories, family recipes, or quiet walks — create lasting memories and instill values like kindness and resilience.

Blending Wisdom with Modern Parenting

Parenting evolves with the times, and combining your experience with contemporary techniques enriches a child's upbringing.

- Stay Curious: Learn modern parenting tools like emotional regulation and positive discipline.
- Bridge Generations: Pair old traditions with fresh ideas. For example:
    - *Traditional Cooking Meets Nutrition: Share recipes while explaining the benefits of balanced meals.*
    - *Mindfulness with Tradition: Combine prayer routines with gratitude journaling to nurture emotional well-being.*
- Be the Connector: Ensure that timeless lessons remain relevant and meaningful in today's world.

THE THIRD SECRET : CELEBRATE

Collaborating with Parents

Your role as a grandparent is to compliment not compete

- Communicate: Regular check-ins help align parenting approaches.
- Respect Boundaries: Honor the parents' choices, even if they differ from your instincts.
- Offer Support: Frame your advice as curiosity, not criticism.

The Beautiful Chaos of Joint Families

A joint family is a dynamic blend of love, tradition, and occasional chaos. With generations living under one roof, it's a unique setup where wisdom, youthful energy, and teamwork flourish.

Why Joint Families Work

- Built-In Support System: From school pickups to bedtime stories, someone's always there to help.
- Wisdom Meets Energy: Grandparents' experience pairs beautifully with the vigor of younger generations.
- Shared Responsibilities: Parenting becomes a collaborative journey, easing the load on everyone.
- Emotional Perspective: Children learn empathy, compromise, and resilience through constant interaction with diverse personalities.

Balancing Traditions and Modernity

Rich traditions coexist beautifully with contemporary parenting styles when approached with openness.

- Celebrate Traditions: Festive rituals, storytelling sessions, and shared meals provide a sense of heritage.
- Innovate Together: Blend old customs with new methods, like turning grandma's hair-oiling into a fun spa day.
- Foster Dialogue: Align generational values by encouraging conversations between older and younger family members.

Mothers, Depression, and Family Dynamics

Research reveals that 72% of mothers face depression after childbirth, often due to family dynamics. When mothers set rules, family members (often in-laws) may undermine them with phrases like "It's okay" or "It doesn't matter."

It results in-
- Confusion: Mixed signals lead to unclear boundaries.
- Lack of Discipline: Kids adapt to inconsistency, causing behavioral challenges.

Key Issues
- Overprotection by In-Laws: Ignoring boundaries creates inconsistency.
- Undermining Authority: Mothers feel unheard, affecting their confidence and mental health.

Navigating the Challenges with Grace

Living with extended family means balancing different perspectives and personalities.

Strategies for Harmony
- Set Clear Boundaries: Define spaces and roles to avoid stepping on toes.

THE THIRD SECRET : CELEBRATE

- Solve Privately: Handle conflicts away from children to maintain a sense of stability.
- Rotate Responsibilities: Share tasks like cooking or homework help to foster collaboration.
- Unified Rules: Family should align with the mother's boundaries.
- Respect the Mother's Role: Empower her decisions to ensure consistency.
- Open Communication: Foster mutual understanding between the mother and in-laws.
- Focus on healthy eating habits as kids are like mirrors and they are copying you blindly.

Figure 30

When It Feels Overwhelming
- Claim Quiet Time: Dedicate 15 minutes for yourself, whether it's reading, meditating, or sipping tea.
- Ask for Help: In a joint family, it's okay to delegate — it's teamwork at its finest!

4.4 GRAND PARENTS AND JOINT FAMILIES

- Focus on Positivity: Celebrate the small moments of joy that make it all worthwhile.

Consistency and respect are essential for your child's balanced development. FAMILY IS ONE UNIT. Give a healthy love. Educating the Family is very important.

But what if society and your family are stuck on patriarchal values? In this case:

1. The mother has to educate herself. Take help from parenting coaches and learn.
2. Once the mother knows the right parenting style, she can stand up for the child and herself.
3. Confidence to first tell the husband that this is what we should do.
4. Then tell the in-laws and speak in a softer tone. No fights are needed, but be firm on, this is how you want to raise kids.
5. Build common family rules – create a mutual agreement on what rules to follow and what can be molded

Kids are smart, they will take advantage of a disbalanced house and will go to different people of the house so that they listen to him and and if mom or dad disagree, they will go to their grandparents.

The Role of Grandparents in a Joint Family

Grandparents are the family's living archives, offering wisdom, stories, and cultural richness.

- Storytime: Share tales of resilience and courage to inspire children.
- Board Games: carrom board, ludo, cards and many more

- Skill Sharing: Teach skills like gardening, cooking, or knitting, creating precious bonding moments.
- Cultural Lessons: Preserve heritage by teaching traditional songs, games, or practices.

Rituals and Celebrations: The Heart of Togetherness

Joint families thrive on shared traditions that deepen bonds and create cherished memories.

Ideas for Shared Rituals

1. Family Game Night: Rotate games to include everyone's favorites.
2. Cultural Days: Explore heritage through stories, crafts, or special meals.
3. Talent Shows: Let family members showcase their skills, from singing to storytelling.

Special Celebrations

- Festivals: Make them grand by involving everyone in decorating, cooking, and rituals.
- Milestones: Celebrate graduations, birthdays, or small wins with family dinners or movie nights.

The Bigger Picture: Growing Up in a Joint Family

For children, life in a joint family offers unique lessons and unshakable bonds.

- Life Skills: They learn teamwork, patience, and the art of compromise.
- Unwavering Support: Someone is always there to cheer them on or offer comfort.

4.4 GRAND PARENTS AND JOINT FAMILIES

- Lifelong Connections: Cousins become lifelong friends, and grandparents remain beloved mentors.

A Final Word to Grandparents and Parents

Dear Caregiver,

Whether you're a grandparent bridging generations or a parent navigating the dynamics of a joint family, your role is invaluable. You're creating a legacy of love, resilience, and togetherness that will echo for generations.

Amid the laughter, shared meals, and occasional debates, remember: you're weaving a story of belonging your children will carry in their hearts forever. Celebrate the chaos, cherish the love, and take pride in the magic you're creating.

You're not just holding it all together — you're making it extraordinary.

CLOSURE

EMBRACING THE PARENTING JOURNEY

As you reach the end of this guide, it's a moment to reflect, recharge, and prepare for the next step in your parenting journey. This book isn't just a collection of advice; it's a resource to revisit, a companion to inspire, and a reminder that you are never alone in this beautiful, challenging, and rewarding experience. Keep going through the strategies and concepts so that "Parenting it Right" comes naturally to you. It's like mathematics, if you practice it daily you will certainly master it.

Final Takeaways

Parenting is about presence, patience, and persistence. Here are the core principles to carry forward:

1. **Connection is Key:** Build a strong emotional bond with children. Whether through shared activities, heartfelt conversations, or simply being present, connection lays the foundation for their confidence and resilience.

2. **Self-Care is Essential:** Your well-being directly influences your parenting. Prioritize yourself without guilt — it's not selfish; it's necessary.
3. **Celebrate the Small Wins:** Parenting is a collection of everyday victories. From surviving bedtime chaos to hearing children say, "Thank you," these moments are worth cherishing.
4. **Balance Boundaries and Freedom:** Provide structure with love, but allow room for exploration and independence. This balance shapes their growth and trust in themselves.
5. **Adapt and Grow Together:** Parenting evolves with children's age and needs. Stay flexible, keep learning, and embrace every stage with an open heart.

What Next?

Parenting is a lifelong adventure, and your journey continues. Here's how to make the most of the lessons and insights you've gained:

1. **Revisit Chapters as Needed:** Whether you're navigating tantrums or teenage milestones, let this book be your go-to guide. Each chapter offers actionable tools you can adapt as children grow.
2. **Join the Community:** Parenting is a collective effort, and you don't have to go it alone. Connect with other parents at www.joyfulparenting.club to share experiences, gain support, and access exclusive resources.
3. **Incorporate What Resonates:** Start with one or two strategies that align with your current parenting goals. Gradually weave them into your daily life for sustainable change.

CLOSURE: EMBRACING THE PARENTING JOURNEY

4. **Sharing is Caring:** Share the book with another parent who might benefit. Parenting is about creating a ripple effect of love, support, and understanding.

A Parting Message

Dear Parent,

You've taken the time to invest in your growth and children's future. That's a profound act of love and I am so, so proud of you. Remember, there's no single "right" way to parent — just the way that works for you and your family.

Embrace the journey with kindness toward yourself and curiosity toward children. Celebrate the moments of joy, laugh through the mishaps, and hold onto the connection that makes parenting so deeply meaningful.

Parenting is a partnership of growth — both yours and children's. With the lessons in this book and your unique love and determination, you're equipped to navigate this incredible journey with confidence and purpose.

Here's to the laughter, love, and legacy you're building. You've got this. 💗

Section 1
What is Parenting

Section 2
The First Secret
Connection

2.1
Foundation Years
1 - 5 Years

2.2
Middle Childhood
6 - 12 Years

2.3
Teenage Years
13 - 18 Years

Section 3
The Second Secret
Care

Section 4
The Third Secret
Celebrate

YOU ARE HERE

Section 5
Parent Survival Kit
50+ Activities

Your Parenting Journey

SECTION 5

PARENT SURVIVAL KIT: 50+ ACTIVITIES

Activities for Parents & Children

5.1 The Foundation Years (1–5 Years)

Chapter 1: Building Emotional Security
- The Connection Jar: Write daily moments of love or gratitude and read them weekly to relive shared joys.
- Safe Space Creation: Set up a comforting area with pillows, blankets, and a favorite toy.

Chapter 2: Raising Curious Explorers
- Curiosity Jar: Capture children's questions and revisit them together.
- Open-Ended Experiment: Provide materials like colors or blocks and let children lead the exploration.

Chapter 3: Play as a Pathway to Growth
- Play Date Reflection: Observe and document their favorite play activities and skills.

- DIY Imagination Box: Fill a box with random household items to inspire creative play.

Chapter 4: Handling Tantrums
- Calm-Down Corner: Designate a soothing space with sensory objects.
- Trigger Tracker: Log tantrum triggers and plan alternative responses.

Chapter 5: Feeding with Love
- Taste Test Adventure: Introduce a new food weekly and encourage descriptive feedback.
- Mealtime Stories: Share fun tales during meals to engage and relax children.

Chapter 6: Sleep Challenges
- Bedtime Visual Chart: Illustrate a bedtime routine for easy understanding.
- Relaxation Practice: Teach deep breathing through playful metaphors like "smelling flowers and blowing out candles."

Chapter 7: Managing Screen Time
- Family Tech Rules Poster: Collaboratively create and decorate screen time guidelines.
- Screen-Free Reward Jar: Use tokens for screen-free activities and trade them for special rewards.

Chapter 8: Navigating Milestones
- Growth Chart Celebration: Mark milestones with stickers and celebrate achievements.
- Weekly Progress Reflection: Note one new skill or activity children tried.

Chapter 9: Balancing Boundaries and Freedom
- Yes/No Choices: Offer simple choices to foster decision-making.
- Boundary Success Log: Celebrate moments when children respected boundaries.

Chapter 10: Celebrating Foundation Years
- Memory Jar: Document beautiful moments weekly, creating a treasure trove of memories.
- Reflect and Adjust Your Boundaries: Analyze boundary challenges and celebrate successes.

5.2 The Middle Childhood (6–12 Years)

Chapter 1: Fostering Independence
- Chore Chart: Assign tasks and track progress with stickers.
- Responsibility Journal: Reflect on their feelings after completing tasks.

Chapter 2: Academic Growth
- Homework Helper Jar: Fill with fun breaks for motivation during study time.
- Weekly Review: Discuss subjects they enjoyed and plan further exploration.

Chapter 3: Emotional Intelligence
- Emotion Matching Game: Use flashcards to associate feelings with scenarios.
- Gratitude Wall: Add daily sticky notes of gratitude.

Chapter 4: Social Skills and Friendships
- Friendship Bingo: Encourage acts of kindness through a playful bingo game.

- Friendship Map: Visualize and reflect on social connections.

Chapter 5: Screen Time and Creativity
- Creative Challenge Calendar: Plan daily creative tasks like art or storytelling.

Chapter 6: Physical and Mental Health
- Eat a Rainbow Every Day- Eat a colorful plate of fruits and veggies daily. Click Pictures and make a scrap file. Do a 21-Day challenge
- Healthy Habits Tracker: Track hydration, exercise, and happy moments daily.
- Mindful Moments: Practice 2 minutes of mindfulness together.

Chapter 7: Nurturing Creativity and Hobbies
- Creative Corner: Dedicate a space for hobbies and creative exploration.

Chapter 8: The Growing Parent-Child Bond
- Conversation Starters Deck: Use open-ended questions to spark meaningful dialogue.

Chapter 9: Introducing Financial Literacy
- Teach children about saving, spending, and Charity. Divide their pocket money into 3

5.3 The Teenage Years (13–18 Years)

Chapter 1: Building Independence
- Responsibility and Reward Chart: Link responsibilities to earned freedoms.

Chapter 2: Emotional Intelligence

PARENT SURVIVAL KIT: 50+ ACTIVITIES

- Weekly Mood Tracker- Spot mood patterns and make positive changes.
- Empathy Map: Explore how actions impact others.

Chapter 3: The Parent-Teen Relationship
- Connection Hour: Spend weekly time doing activities your teen enjoys.
- Compliment Exchange: Share what you appreciate about each other.

Chapter 4: Career Guidance
- Career Exploration Chart: Link interests to potential career paths.

Chapter 5: Social Dynamics
- Peer Influence Worksheet: Reflect on peer interactions and choices.

Chapter 6: Screen Time, Social Media, and Digital Boundaries
- Digital Reset Challenge: Reduce non-productive screen time and replace it with enriching activities.

Chapter 7: Physical and Mental Health
- The Wellness Wheel: Rate satisfaction in key areas like sleep and nutrition, and set improvement goals.

Chapter 8: Sexuality, Relationships, and Safety
- The Relationship Bar Graph: Evaluate and discuss trust, respect, and communication in relationships.

Chapter 9: Fostering Creativity and Passion Projects
- Passion Pie Chart: Identify and pursue interests and hobbies.

Chapter 10: Preparing for Adulthood

- Life Skills Checklist: Assess confidence in essential skills like budgeting and time management.

5.4 Self-Care for Parents

- Gratitude Journal: Write three things you're grateful for daily.
- Pause and Pivot Toolkit: Identify stress triggers and practice reflective responses.
- Micro Self-Care Menu: Commit to small daily self-care actions like stretching or journaling.

5.5 Diverse Parenting Situations

Single Parenting
- Support Network Planner: List trusted people and schedule weekly check-ins.

Co-Parenting After Divorce
- Conflict-Free Zone: Create a positive-only communication space about the co-parent.

Sibling Rivalry
- Sibling Jar: Write down fun activities (like building forts or making pancakes) and pick one when tensions rise.
- Turn-Taking Cards: Create a system for sharing high-demand items, like favorite games or devices.
- Kindness Chart: Track acts of kindness between siblings, rewarding them for cooperation and care.

Grandparents as Caregivers
- Family Legacy Project: Document recipes, stories, or traditions with children.

PARENT SURVIVAL KIT: 50+ ACTIVITIES

Family Traditions and Rituals
- Seasonal Celebration Planner: Create checklists for festive traditions.
- Family Tree Project: Build a tree with stories and photos.

This Parent Survival Kit ensures parents have practical, actionable activities to navigate every stage of their child's growth while fostering joy, connection, and balance in their parenting journey. 💞

SECTION 6

20+ STRATEGIES FOR SMART PARENTING

Practical Tips for Every Age & Stage

*E*ach one is designed to help parents foster a positive and nurturing environment for their children, making the parenting journey smoother and more fulfilling.

1. The Golden Hour – BONDING ACTIVITY

1 Hour before sleep the child's brain goes into theta mode and the yes brain is activated so bonding at that time is very important. This strategy focuses on bonding before bedtime to nurture emotional security. Share stories, talk about your day, or give affirmations like, "You made me so proud today." This approach strengthens the parent-child bond and fosters a sense of safety and love, crucial for healthy attachment and emotional development.

2. Pause and Pivot- THINK AND REACT

Based on Dr. Daniel Siegel's work on emotional regulation, this technique emphasizes responding calmly to challenging behavior. Instead of reacting impulsively, pause, identify children's emotions, and address them with empathy. For example, say, "I see you're upset. Let's figure it out together." This promotes trust, emotional intelligence, and self-control.

3. The Power of Words- The HIDDEN MESSAGE IN WATER

Dr. Masaru Emoto's research on how words affect water crystals reveals that positive language has transformative power. Since our bodies are 75% water, encouraging words like "You're amazing!" can shape confidence and self-esteem. Replace criticism with affirmations to build children's resilience and emotional health.

4. Porcupine quills = Kids Tantrums

<u>Concept created by me</u> 😊 -This approach highlights that tantrums are a child's way of expressing emotional overload. Like a porcupine raising its quills, children use tantrums to protect themselves. Staying calm and validating their feelings ("I see you're frustrated") teaches emotional regulation while maintaining their trust.

5. The 7x7 Connection Rule

<u>Concept created by me</u> 😊 - Emphasize on the power of small daily interactions, this strategy suggests creating seven 7-minute moments of connection each day. Morning hugs, bedtime chats, and quick after-school check-ins help children feel valued and loved, even in a busy schedule.

6. Chores for Champions – LIFE SKILLS

Based on the Montessori method, assigning age-appropriate chores helps children develop life skills, independence, and responsibility. Starting with simple tasks like picking up toys and progressing to cooking meals equips them for adulthood while boosting confidence and teamwork.

0–3 Years- Builds early habits of contribution. Pick up toys, put clothes in the laundry basket, wipe small spills.

4–5 Years- Teaches basic organization skills. Make the bed (with help), water plants, sort socks, set the table.

6–8 Years- Encourages independence and motor skills. Feed pets, dust furniture, fold laundry, help with meal prep.

9–12 Years- Builds confidence and self-reliance. Vacuum, take out trash, prepare snacks, tidy room.

13–15 Years- Prepares teens for responsibilities. Do laundry, clean bathrooms, mow the lawn, cook meals.

16–19 Years- Equips young adults for independent living. Cook family meals, handle grocery shopping, manage schedules, assist with household maintenance.

7. Yes-No-YES Framework

This approach validates a child's feelings while setting boundaries. Instead of saying, "No, you can't play," reframe it as, "Yes, I see you want to play, and we need to eat dinner first. Let's play afterward." This builds cooperation and respect for rules without conflict.

8. Healthy Screen Time Guidelines

Concept: Backed by the American Academy of Pediatrics (AAP), this strategy ensures screen use is balanced and purposeful. For example:

- 0–18 months: Video chats only.
- 2–5 years: Max 1 hour/day of educational content.
- 6–10 years: 1–2 hours/day balanced with active play.
- 11–19 years: Self-regulated, with focus on academics and hobbies.
- Creating screen-free zones (e.g., during meals) helps children maintain healthy habits.

9. A Creative Corner

Setting up a dedicated space with art supplies and puzzles encourages unstructured exploration. This stimulates imagination, problem-solving skills, and cognitive development while providing a constructive outlet for energy.

10. Lunchbox Love Notes

Rooted in the idea of emotional deposits "Emotional Bank Account", writing small notes like "You'll do great today!" boosts children's confidence and sense of security. These simple gestures remind them of your love even when you're apart.

11. The Pomodoro Focus Technique

Francesco Cirillo's time-management method, the Pomodoro Technique, helps children manage focus and breaks effectively.

Setting a timer for 25 minutes of work followed by a 5-minute break makes homework less overwhelming and improves productivity.

Tip: Before kids start studying use the Binaural Brain Boost. It enhances child's focus during study sessions by playing 40 Hz binaural beats for five minutes beforehand. These auditory tones stimulate both sides of the brain, improving concentration and cognitive function, making learning more effective. You can find the beats on YouTube.

12. Tap & Calm Technique (EFT)

Emotional Freedom Technique (EFT), developed by Gary Craig, involves tapping on pressure points like the forehead, top of the head, under the eyes, on the chin, on the collar bone and so on while repeating calming affirmations like "I am safe." This method reduces stress, helping children and parents manage anxiety and overwhelming emotions.

13. The Emotion Compass

Marc Brackett's RULER framework, the full form of RULER is:
- R: Recognizing emotions
- U: Understanding emotions
- L: Labeling emotions
- E: Expressing emotions
- R: Regulating emotions

This helps in identifying emotions and builds emotional awareness, a key skill for emotional intelligence. This tool teaches children to recognize emotions using colors:

- Red = Anger
- Blue = Sadness
- Green = Calmness
- Yellow = Happiness

14. Tech Diet Design

Research on screen time compares technology use to a balanced diet. Divide screen time into "nourishment" (learning, creativity) and "treats" (gaming, Netflix). Involving children in creating this balance fosters self-regulation and healthy habits.

15. The Sleep Sync- Teenage Sleep

Studies by the National Sleep Foundation reveal that teenagers need 8–10 hours of sleep, yet most don't get enough due to biological shifts and late-night habits. Encourage a consistent bedtime routine and limit screens an hour before bed to improve rest and overall well-being. So, when your teen sleeps longer celebrate it because your teen's brain is developing for good.

16. The 4D Time Triage

Inspired by productivity expert David Allen, it reduces stress and teaches prioritization. This strategy helps children and parents manage their time effectively:

1. Delete unnecessary tasks.
2. Delegate to others.
3. Defy perfectionism.
4. Do one thing at a time.

17. Hug It Out

Family therapist Virginia Satir emphasized that "we need 4 hugs a day for survival, 8 for maintenance, and 12 for growth." Regular hugs release oxytocin, the bonding hormone, strengthening emotional connection and reducing stress for both children and parents.

18. The Gratitude Tree or Family Gratitude Book

Creating a family gratitude tree or book helps visualize shared appreciation. Write something you're thankful for on a paper leaf each day and add it to the tree. Over time, it becomes a beautiful reminder of your family's blessings. Perfect family bonding activity.

19. Decluttering Together

Decluttering teaches that a tidy space creates a calmer mind. Make it fun by setting a timer for 15 minutes and turning it into a family game. A clutter-free environment fosters focus and peace. You can practically declutter – by uninstalling apps, digital decluttering, home decluttering. Brain decluttering is also equally important to remove toxic thoughts from your mind It is necessary to "Forget and Forgive" for decluttering so that you can start fresh and happy.

20. 2:2:2 Family Rule

This Strengthens relationships, breaks routine, and brings everyone closer. Simple, intentional, and effective!

4. Every 2 Weeks: Go on a date night with your partner — keep the spark alive!

5. Every 2 Months: Plan a family outing or day trip — bond over fun adventures.
6. Every 2 Years: Take a family vacation — create memories to last a lifetime.

These 20 strategies are practical and adaptable, helping parents nurture their child's emotional intelligence, confidence, and resilience while building a loving and supportive family environment.

"Give Your Child Wings" encourages parents to nurture their child's emotional intelligence, independence, and resilience while rediscovering joy in their own role. Blending timeless principles with modern insights, it equips parents to build a legacy of love, connection, and positive growth for their children and themselves.

SUMMARY

GIVE YOUR CHILD WINGS

The Ultimate Parenting Guide

This book, authored by Swati Gupta, is a comprehensive parenting guide that focuses on fostering deep, meaningful connections between parents and children while navigating the complexities of modern life. It emphasizes practical strategies and tools to create a nurturing, balanced, and joyful family environment.

Core Themes of the Book

1. **The 4 Pillars of Parenting:**
   - **Connection:** *Prioritizing time and emotional presence to build trust and safety.*
   - **Consistency:** *Establishing routines that provide stability and discipline.*
   - **Compassion:** *Empathizing with your child's emotions to foster resilience.*
   - **Communication:** *Keeping dialogue open to nurture understanding and emotional intelligence.*

SUMMARY

2. The 3 Secrets of Parenting:
- **Connect:** *Building trust and emotional bonds with your child through intentional moments and presence. "Connection is Above Correction"*
- **Care:** *Embracing self-care as a vital aspect of parenting, ensuring parents model balance and well-being. "Self-Care is Self Ishq and not Selfish"*
- **Celebrate:** *Acknowledging small and big wins, and cherishing the unique journey of every family. "Happy Parents = Happy Child = Happy Family"*

Structure of the Book

1. Introduction:
- *The book begins with the author's personal parenting journey, highlighting the transformative power of intentional parenting.*
- *It provides practical tools and reflections for overcoming guilt, managing digital distractions, and fostering meaningful family connections.*

2. Detailed Parenting Strategies by Age Groups:
- **Foundation Years (1–5 years):** *Focuses on building emotional security, managing tantrums, and establishing early routines.*
- **Middle Childhood (6–12 years):** *Divided into 2 parts Early Growth Years (6 to 8 years) and Pre-teen years (9 to 12 years). Guides parents in nurturing independence, fostering creativity, and balancing academic growth with emotional intelligence.*

- **Teenage Years (13–19 years):** *Addresses the challenges of adolescence, including social dynamics, screen time, and preparing for adulthood.*

3. **Practical Tools and Activities:**
   - **Golden Nuggets:** *Actionable parenting tips like "7 Slots of 7 Minutes," DEAR Time (Drop Everything and Read), "Power of Words- Hidden message of Water" and creating "Connection Jars."*
   - **Survival Kit:** *Over 50 activities and 20+ strategies to strengthen family bonds and handle everyday parenting challenges.*
   - **Routines:** *Ideas for bedtime rituals, Golden hour parenting, mealtime traditions, and transition strategies to create a sense of security and belonging.*

4. **Modern Challenges and Solutions:**
   - *Addresses the digital age's impact on parenting, including screen time management, emotional regulation, and fostering real-world connections.*

5. **Special Topics:**
   - *Single parenting, co-parenting after divorce, sibling relationships, and the role of extended families are explored with empathy and actionable advice.*

Key Takeaways

- **Connection is Above Correction:** A connected child is more likely to thrive emotionally and socially than one who feels overly corrected.

SUMMARY

- **Parenting Requires Growth:** By evolving as a parent, you model resilience, curiosity, and emotional intelligence for your children.
- **Small Moments Matter:** Everyday interactions, even as brief as 7 minutes, can significantly strengthen the parent-child bond.
- **Self-Care is Key:** A happy and balanced parent creates a happier family environment.

"Give Your Child Wings" is not just a guide but an invitation for parents to embark on a transformative journey of growth, understanding, and joy. By combining actionable tips, relatable anecdotes, and research-based strategies, the book equips parents to raise resilient, confident, and connected children.

Do take a moment to share this book with your spouse, your friends or extended family members, if you feel this could help them as well. Parenting is complex and I believe that it would benefit every parent to deepen their understanding of child psychology and build self-awareness. If you feel this book has made a difference in your life, I will urge you to gift it to at least one parent with the intent of supporting them in their parenting journey. My ultimate goal is to create a community of joyful, happy parents and with your help. I want to reach out to as many parents out there as possible! Let us all live a fulfilling life with our kids and family.

ABOUT JOYFUL PARENTING CLUB

While teaching creative writing to students, I began interacting with parents and realised that they were facing challenges similar to those I faced as a mother. Over time, I spoke with more than 2000 parents, which fueled my passion for helping them build strong, meaningful bonds with their children and achieve a fulfilled family life.

As a mother of two and an educator with over 10 years of experience, I've guided parents, shared parenting tips on my social handles (@parenting_swati), and conducted extensive research in child psychology and parenting. These experiences inspired me to create the Joyful Parenting Club — a thriving online community and safe space for parents.

The Joyful Parenting Club is designed with a deep understanding of the challenges modern parents face. It's a place where you'll find support, encouragement, and inspiration to thrive as a parent while

ABOUT JOYFUL PARENTING CLUB

prioritizing your own well-being. Here, there is no judgment — only understanding, guidance, and the tools to create joy, balance, and confidence in your parenting journey. I

Inside Joyful Parenting Club, you'll get:

- Parenting masterclass & workshops for tackling different parenting challenges
- Practical tools, courses and strategies tailored to your parenting goals.
- A judgment-free platform to share struggles and celebrate wins.
- A network of parents who lift each other up, like lifelong companions and cheerleaders.

You're not just joining any club — you're becoming part of an exclusive community that genuinely cares about helping you find joy in every step of your parenting journey.

I invite you to join my parenting community "Joyful Parenting Club" and begin your journey with me today. Together, let's make parenting a joyful and fulfilling experience! Join now: www.joyfulparenting.club

Scan QR Code Above to Know More

"Cheers to Joyful Parenting! 🤗"

"-Swati Gupta"

ACKNOWLEDGMENTS

This book is not just a collection of words — it is my heart laid bare. It would never have been possible without the love and strength of the incredible people who make my life whole.

To my husband, Mohit — my rock, my partner in everything — I can never thank you enough for standing by my side, cheering me on, and lifting me up on the days when I doubted myself. Your belief in me, even when I couldn't see it in myself, has been the wind beneath my wings. You've always been my silent hero. Thank you for holding me steady as I followed my passion.

To my little (but mighty) cuties, Ashwika and Ribhav — you've been my greatest teachers and inspirations. Your endless questions, big feelings, and boundless energy have taught me more about parenting than any book or course ever could. Watching you grow, stumble, and rise again has been the greatest joy of my life. This book holds pieces of you in every word, and I hope you know just how much I love you.

To my mom, Sarita — my forever guiding star — even though you're no longer here, I feel your presence with me every single day. Your love, values, and quiet strength are woven into the fabric of who I am. I know you're still watching over me, cheering me

ACKNOWLEDGMENTS

on from above. I miss you every day, but I know your blessings make all of this possible. To my dad, Mahendra– for always being by my side and blessing me in all my endeavors.

To my mother-in-law, Shashi, my pillar of support, from the time I got married till the time she was around. Your words of wisdom have stayed with me and will stay with me forever. To my father-in-law, Lalit– whose heavenly presence has always been there with me since I got married.

To my sister-in-law, Richa– my constant support system and soul sister– you've always been with me through the thick and thin of life, standing in front of me, rather behind.

And to every parent who has trusted me with their struggles, shared their stories, and followed me along on this journey– your courage and honesty have given me purpose and inspired every page of this book.

This book is a labor of love and a testament to the people who have shaped me, stood by me, and believed in me. From the bottom of my heart, thank you for being my family, my inspiration, and my reason to keep going. This journey wouldn't have been possible without you.

ABOUT THE AUTHOR

Swati Gupta
Founder, Joyful Parenting Club

Swati Gupta is an Educationist, Parenting Coach and Founder of Joyful Parenting Club & Atusy.com. She wears many hats—a wife, a mother, a creative writing coach, a storyteller, a podcast host of *"Wisdom Waves"*, an Instagrammer with over 900 videos, a YouTuber and a motivational speaker. Through her work, Swati has touched the lives of countless families, inspiring them to embrace the joys and imperfections of parenting.

She has been featured on Josh Talks. Through her Instagram profile @parenting_swati, she connects with a vibrant community of over 50,000 parents, sharing parenting tips, tricks, and moments of inspiration. She has a Bachelor's in Education and is a Montessori expert in child psychology. She loves kids and has over a decade of teaching experience at India's most reputed schools.

She's passionate about helping parents create a 100% bond with their child and live a fulfilled family life. Her journey as a mother of two, combined with her professional background and years of

ABOUT THE AUTHOR

research on Parenting, inspired her to create the *Joyful Parenting Club*. This thriving community helps parents find joy, balance, and confidence in raising their children.

Her philosophy?

Parenting is all about "CONNECTION ABOVE CORRECTION"!

Through her workshops, online content, and this book, she offers compassionate and practical advice to parents. She also helps parents become parenting coaches and life coaches. She has guided countless children as a creative writing coach to help them write their stories and poems; many have published their own books.

Born and raised in the culturally rich city of Kolkata, she brings a unique blend of personal and professional experience to her work. As a mother of two delightful children, aged 13 and 6 (when writing this book), Swati has walked the path of parenting herself and understands the joys and challenges it entails. With over a decade of teaching experience at leading schools, her insights enable her to effectively guide parents and children toward stronger connections and more fulfilling relationships.

This book holds a special place for her as it reflects her journey as a parent and coach. It is inspired by the lessons she learned while raising her children and supporting countless families through her workshops and online community. Swati believes parenting is a beautiful balance of connection, patience, and learning.

Swati is deeply grateful to every reader of this book. She is confident that it will help you celebrate the little moments, cherish the beauty in imperfection, and nurture the precious bond you

ABOUT THE AUTHOR

share with your child. She wants to reach as many parents as possible through this book. This book is an invitation to join her in embracing the joys and messiness of parenting while giving your child the wings to fly.

You can connect with Swati and explore more of her work here:

- Instagram: bit.ly/parentingswatiinsta
- WhatsApp: bit.ly/joyfulparentingwhatsapp
- YouTube: bit.ly/parentingswatiyoutube
- Website: www.joyfulparenting.club
- Joyful Parenting Podcast: spoti.fi/40jfa7R

RESOURCES

*H*ere is the list of essential resources which will help you in your parenting journey.

S.no	Resources	Resource Type	QR Code	Links
1	Exclusive Parenting Group	Join WhatsApp Group		bit.ly/WhatsappBook
2	Parenting Masterclass	Register for the Masterclass		bit.ly/JPCmasterclass
3	Joyful Parenting Club	Check the Website		bit.ly/Joyfulparenting
4	121 Session	Book 121 session with me		bit.ly/JPC121session
5	E-Book on Building Confidence	Download the E-Book		bit.ly/JPbuildconfidence
6	A Parent Guide on Sex Education	Download the E-Book		bit.ly/JPSexeducation

RESOURCES

7	Parent Survival Kit	50 + Activities		bit.ly/giveyourchildwings
8	What Stories to Narrate?	Blog on Story Telling		bit.ly/7minutestorytelling
9	Book Recommendations	Blog on DEAR Time		bit.ly/DearTimeBlog
10	Age-Wise Affirmations	Blog on Affirmations		bit.ly/affirmationsagewise
11	Calming Technique for kids	50 Calming Activities for Kids		bit.ly/JPC50CalmingActivities
12	Milestones for Children	Life Skills for 0 to 18 years		bit.ly/Familyblissblog1
13	Joyful Parenting App	Download iOS App		bit.ly/JoyfulParentingAppIOS
14	Joyful Parenting App	Download Android App		bit.ly/joyfulparentingclub
15	Weekly Newsletter	Subscribe to the Newsletter		bit.ly/JPCNewsletter
16	Blogs	Follow the Blog Page		bit.ly/JPCBlogs

DISCLOSURE

*T*his book is intended to serve as a supportive guide for parents navigating the joys and challenges of raising children. The information, advice, and strategies shared are drawn from personal experiences, professional training, and research in child development and parenting. While every effort has been made to ensure the accuracy and relevance of the content, it is important to recognize that parenting is a deeply personal journey, and what works for one family may not work for another.

The ideas and suggestions provided in this book are not a substitute for professional medical, psychological, or legal advice. If you have concerns about children's health, development, or well-being, please seek guidance from a qualified professional.

Parenting is deeply influenced by culture, traditions, religion, caste, societal expectations and any of the other belief systems. These strategies are not meant to hurt any sentiments or feelings towards any of these. Nothing contained in this book has direct reference to any of these and does not refer to any person directly, dead or alive. Any resemblance is purely coincidental and not at all intentional. These are the author's own experiences and creative expressions.

DISCLOSURE

All copyrights, trademarks and work referenced from other authors; publishers & creators belong to the respective intellectual property owners. We claim no right to the content or design that belongs to them. All referenced content is used in good faith to impart meaningful concepts to parents to help them benefit in their parenting journey. References have been provided wherever available and as much practically possible. No references have been missed out intentionally.

The author disclaim any liability for outcomes resulting from the application of the information presented in this book. Every family is unique, and we encourage you to consult the appropriate qualified professional depending on your unique circumstances and situations.

Every individual is different and reader should use anything from this book at their sole discretion. If you are not sure on anything, and cannot take responsibility for your own actions or decisions, kindly do not refer or use anything presented in this book.

This book is designed only to inspire, support, and empower you on your parenting journey, and nothing beyond that.

www.ingramcontent.com/pod-product-compliance
Lightning Source LLC
LaVergne TN
LVHW091715070526
838199LV00050B/2407